Introduction

It's almost hard to even find a place to start this book. Steven and I have been thru so much on this journey, there is so much I want to share, and to write, so I will do my best as I go along. Thru the years, I have met so many parents and children who are going thru so many of the same things that we have experienced; I have always been the first to share our story with others. I realized that maybe I could help someone who is new to LGS, who has all of the same questions that I had when Steven was first diagnosed. In the 15 years I have been living with epilepsy thru my son, I still don't have all the answers that so many other parents are searching for. I had always thought that epilepsy was just when you fall on the floor, like an unexpected earthquake, and then get up and you're fine. I had no idea of the many medicines that there are to treat epilepsy. Most of all, I never knew how many children suffer with this disorder. In my life I would have never expected this whirlwind of emotions, heartbreaks, and pain that I would have to try to overcome. I never knew there were syndromes to go along with epilepsy, and worst of all I had no idea about Lennox Gastaut Syndrome. I have even met doctors who don't know what LGS is. There were so many things that I was not informed of, that I had to learn from others, and there were no social networking sites when Steven was first diagnosed, so I was basically on my own. I am not by all means, an expert, but I am a mom, and a mother that has been going thru this for fifteen long years. We have been thru medications, surgeries, diets, most everything that goes with LGS. I hope that if I can help just one person, then this as all worth it. This is the story of my sweet boy, and a young mother, and an ugly disease, with no ending, but hopefully someday I can say that there is a cure.

A little about me

I am just going to start at the beginning, from when I first experienced a person with a disability. I remember that I was in elementary school, only in kindergarten. There was a school in back of the kindergarten playground for disabled children and we usually had recess at the same time as the kids at that school. My friends and I would be out there and make fun of those kids, we saw them as different from us, even at that young age, we saw that they were not "normal" like us. Their weird helmets, that looked like old fashioned football gear, the way they were always smiling, like they just didn't have a clue, the loud strange noises they would make. I just knew something wasn't right with them, again, I was only 5. As I grew up, I was still in the same elementary school. I would see the "retarded" kids on their little yellow busses and still, I just knew they weren't like me, I was better than them. I don't think the reality hit me until I was in Jr. High school doing a Choir performance. We were doing a Christmas show and one of the places we had to perform was at that school with the little yellow school busses. I wasn't looking forward to it, and I will admit, my friends and I were still making fun of the disabled kids. We arrived at the school and stood in our lineup we were assigned to for our performance. I was nervous and didn't know what to expect, I didn't think the kids would even be able to enjoy our singing, I thought we were wasting our time. The kids started coming into the multipurpose room, they were wearing their helmets, some in wheelchairs, and some kids even looked older than I was. Each child came in with the biggest smile on their face, like they were just happy to see us! The kids with Downs Syndrome stood out the most to me. Their smiles were the biggest. As we began to sing, tears started filling my eyes, I had to hold them back. The kids were clapping for us, smiling, unlike any audience we had ever had before. When we were finished with our performance, some of the kids gave us hugs, and I noticed I wasn't the only one crying. It was something I will never forget, ever. Over the years, I still had that prejudice about the kids on the little yellow bus, even with that experience I had. I would tell my friends "I will never have a kid on the "Twinkie bus", as we all called it. Little did I know.

Life went on, and it was pretty normal as far as a teenagers life. I had my friends, my favorite bands and even still played with my Barbies from time to time. It took me a while to grow up, I guess. When I was about 19 years old I found out that my mother was very sick, it was the beginning of my never ending visits to the hospital, an being a caregiver, I really had no idea what was in store for me. My mom had been very sick, and my family and I had just figured that she had some kind of virus. She had gained quite a bit of weight and again, we just thought she was eating to much, I even told her to stop eating so much ice cream! I don't really remember why she finally went to the hospital, but she did and we found out she had cirrhosis of the liver and it was not good news. Her local doctor sent her to a university in Los Angeles for treatment. I remember the first time I went there with her, the Liver transplant team wanted the family to come to a meeting to be informed about her condition. The place was so huge; I had never seen a hospital as large as this. I have to admit, I was looking for movie stars while I was there, hey, it was Los Angeles, actually closer to Beverly Hills. I was star struck. I didn't see any celebrities, and the visits continued for another 4 years. My mom went thru absolute pain and misery. My younger sister and I had to clean up her mess when she couldn't make it to the toilet, we had to make sure she ate the right foods, and worse, we had to hear her cry almost daily. It's such a difficult situation to really even describe, because you want them out of pain yet you don't want them to leave. I can still see her to this day like it was yesterday, the physical changes to her from this disease killing her slowly. Her legs would turn purple from the poison in her body, her face was so sunken in and grey. All of us kids knew she was going to die, she knew she was going to die. She tried to prepare us for it, in her silly ways that she had. My mom loved to make everyone smile and she was the first to be the comedian. I don't know if she actually thought my sister and I would actually do what she said, but we did. One day she was lying on the couch and told us girls to come over and put her makeup on. We agreed and as we were making her pretty she said "Pretend that I am dead so you and Danielle will be prepared to do my makeup when I go". She wanted us girls to do her makeup when she passed. We thought she was kidding, and laughed at her saying "ya right, ok mom!" She continued to go in and out of the hospital, so many times we thought that she wouldn't be home and "this was it" that when she did finally pass away, we didn't expect it. The night before she passed, I had taken Steven to a doctor's appointment at a hospital in Orange County. I returned home after a very long day to see that my mother had a bruise on her thigh, and then another on her inner leg. She said it was nothing, that she had bumped herself on the dresser, but I didn't believe it. My dad and I put Steven in the car and drove her to the hospital. She was bleeding internally; I assume it was from her liver. She seemed fine though, laughing and even begging me to let her hold Steven. He was sleeping and I didn't want to wake him so I told her "no mom, you will see him in the morning" I will forever regret those words and my stubbornness. That morning never came for her. We received a phone call the next morning that we needed to come back as soon as possible, that there wasn't much time left. My family arrived there and my sister and I went in to her room. She was in the Intensive Care Unit so I couldn't bring Steven in. My mom was pretty much out of it, but my sister and I were able to somewhat talk to her, I don't remember what we even said but I remember we did talk and tell her that we loved her. My sister fed her some Jell-O and we decided to let her rest for a while we went over to my grandma's house for a bit. Again, another phone call and we had to go right back to the hospital. This time, my mom was in a coma. She passed away around 7 pm. My sister was screaming and crying; I just gave my son to my grandma and ran into her room. My family and I threw everyone else out and it was just the 3 of us, my dad, me and my brother and sister. I was shaking my mom and yelling "mommy, wake up". I will never forget my little brothers big blue eyes with tears in them. The tears made his eyes look like a crystal blue ocean. She was gone, and she went so fast. We had always assumed every time she was in the hospital that she would be home just like every other time, but this was the reality, it was over. I didn't want to live, and honestly, if it hadn't been for my son, Steven, I don't know what would have happened to me. I had to be strong for him and for that reason I think God had everything planned, he knew what I would need to get me thru it all. I thought I would never go thru anything that hard ever again. Me and my sister did do her makeup, and I have that image of my mom in the casket, gray and cold in my mind forever. I wanted to share this experience which really seems like it has nothing to do with my son or LGS, and it doesn't, but I wanted to share how my mind was, how I thought this was the worst thing in my life to ever happen to me. How I never thought I would be able to go thru life without her, yet I had no idea what God had in store for me. I didn't know that I was going have to be the strongest I had to be in my life in years to come. I was so naive back then. I'm not saying that I don't miss her, and that this wasn't a traumatic event in my life, but this was LIFE, something that everyone will go thru at some point in time. It's the things that are so unexpected and unusual that you have to go thru that are the ones that live with you forever and truly change your life.

Having my son, the journey begins

I have to back up a little to get to the birth of my son, but every detail is important and I don't want to leave out anything. Hopefully it's not so confusing, but I will do the best I can. I was 2 when I found out I was pregnant with Steven. I was happy, but at the same time scared to death. I really didn't want to have kids, as I was so young still and I was going to be a single mother. I knew how to care for a baby, as I pretty much raised my brother and sister, but one of my own was more responsibility. I knew I had my mom to help me so it was a little relief knowing she was there, although she was sick, I still had her. I carried Steven to full term, and I had a very easy pregnancy. I never had morning sickness, and I didn't even look pregnant!! I remember when I was 9 months, people were in shock that I was so far along, I was wearing size 9 jeans, and I just got lucky I guess. I went to all of my doctor appointments weekly and when I was close to my due date, my doctor ordered a non-stress test, I don't know why I was asked to do that particular test, but I went in and to get it done. My mom was with me and the nurses hooked up a heart monitor to my tummy so they could monitor Stevens's heartbeat. It seemed like I was there forever, I even started crying at one point because I just wanted to have my baby. The nurses kept coming in and telling me I had to stay a little while longer, nobody ever told me why, and I really didn't worry, I figured there was a good reason, but I wasn't thinking it was anything bad. After about 2 hours, the nurse came in and said that the doctor called and they were going to induce labor. I didn't understand. The nurse explained to me that Stevens's heart rate wasn't going as high as a baby's heartbeat should be. She said that as a precaution he needed to come out. I have to admit, I was so excited, but a little scared at the same time, as I had no idea what to expect. The nurse took me to another room where I was to deliver Steven.

After a while, she came in and had to break my water since it didn't do it on its own. That's when the pain started. Until then, I thought having a baby was a piece of cake!! The contractions were so hard and painful, I don't think I have ever felt pain like that in my life. It felt as if my whole body was ripping itself apart. I was in that room for 8 hours and all the while, Stevens heart rate was still abnormal. The nurse came in and told me that the doctor was on her way and that they were going to have to do a cesarean due to his heart rate. After 8 hours?? NOW you are going to do this?? At the time, I didn't think anything of it. I was just glad that he was going to be born and that I was going to see his little face! I think my biggest worry was that he didn't look like his dad! My mom was in the operating room with me, she had to wear a blue gown and hat to be in there, I guess to be sanitary. They gave me an epidural and Steven was born at midnight exactly. He was a little guy, 5lbs 13oz 18in long. My mom held him before me, and I got to I kiss his little forehead before they gave me a shot to knock me out. I didn't see him until the next morning. Everything was fine, he had 5 fingers and 5 toes and he was beautiful. Back then, the nursery cared for the babies so the mommies could rest, but I liked to have him with me as much as possible. He had big beautiful blue eyes, and was just perfect, I was in love immediately. He was my little twin, I got my wish I guess, and I was happy that he looked just like his mommy. We stayed in the hospital for 2 days and were sent home, nice and healthy. Nothing to worry about.

A new kind of life

I was so glad to be home, but I was in so much pain from the surgery, as well as being a new mom, I was exhausted. My younger brother and sister lived at home as well as my mother, so I was very fortunate to have the help. The second night home, I was so tired that I was almost delirious. My mom begged me to let her take care of Steven for the night so I could get some rest, I was hesitant because I knew she was sick, but I agreed and I slept so well that night!! The next morning, when I woke up, my mom said that Steven didn't eat much that night. I didn't think too much of it, as I was still unfamiliar with this new little guy, I just figured it was because I wasn't with him and didn't seem to concerned. It was later in the day, when I went to give him his bath and I noticed he wasn't crying, which was not like him, he HATED his baths. I laid him on the bed and he just laid there, not really moving much. I knew something was wrong. I asked my dad if what he thought and he said that it was probably nothing. My aunt was there and she too said that it was probably nothing, that he was probably just getting used to being home. I just had that feeling, I had to make sure he was alright. My cousin was at my house and I asked him to take me to the ER, my mom went with me. Funny, looking back, I still remember the seat we sat in in the ER room, even the room Steven was seen in. Anyways, the ER doctors admitted him immediately and ran some tests since he was a newborn. My mom told me to go home and get some sleep, she would stay there in the hospital with him. Again, I felt bad because she was sick herself, but I went home because I knew that I was no good for my baby if I didn't get rest. My mom called about 4 hours later and said I should get back to the hospital immediately. Stevens's blood glucose was at 2. Normal was 40 or higher. He almost didn't make it. I got to the hospital and had to be put in a wheelchair because I couldn't even breathe , let alone walk from my recent cesarean. I was hyperventilating, Stevens pediatrician, who had also been my pediatrician told me to calm down and reassured me that she was doing everything she could. She told me that she called a children's hospital that was about 30 minutes away and an ambulance was on its way to come and get Steven. I can still see it when I close my eyes, the dark night, the red lights of the ambulance and them driving away with my baby. I want sure if I would ever see him again.

  Steven was admitted to the NICU there. I arrived at the hospital the very next morning along with my parents. I remember that before you could even enter the NICU you had to scrub your hands and arms for 5 minutes with this orange antibacterial soap and a course scrub brush. He was in his own little room surrounded by several other little rooms with newborns in them. The room was pretty much empty, except for a blue fold out chair, a crib and a rocking chair. I didn't like the nurses there, I felt as if they were trying to take my baby away, I wasn't used to all the in depth questions they were asking. Because I was so young, and looked even younger than my age, I was afraid that they all thought I wasn't fit to be a mother, or maybe somehow blamed me for him being there. I just hugged my mom and cried, I hated being there, I hated my son being there, and I just wanted to go home. We met with a cardiologist that day, as well as so many other doctors. I think the worst part was when the cardiologist told me that he was going to have to operate on Stevens heart. He explained that a part of his heart was like a "hose", well, there was kink in the hose and the blood wasn't flowing properly. I asked him if Steven was going to die, the doctor replied "Well ,everyone dies at some time". I couldn't believe he had the nerve to tell me something like that!! I went home that night and my family all prayed. That's all we could do and I believed that God would give me a miracle. We called a couple of pastors we knew, and we just prayed. That was all I had. Before returning to the hospital the next day, I stopped by my grandma's house, which was on the way. My grandma mentioned to me "well, at least we have some pictures of him". I was not giving up that easily. I was not going to just have pictures, I was going to bring my son home! When we returned to the hospital, the cardiologist came in and said "I don't know what happened, but the kink in his heart is gone"! I said "it was the Lord!" he then replied in a stern, unfeeling voice "again, I don't know what happened, but it is gone." I KNOW what happened. It took another long three weeks for the hospital to get Stevens blood sugar under control. Steven didn't want to eat much, so we had to just do tiny amounts of formula with a sugar solution at a time. It wasn't even ounces he was drinking at a time, it was more like ml's. Slowly he started eating, getting to about 2 oz every 3 hours. He had so many pokes in his little hands, legs and even in his forehead when they couldn't get to his tiny veins in his arms anymore. It was hard, but during those three weeks, I am so thankful for that time I got to spend with my mom. She stayed with me at the Ronald Mc Donald house, it was a place they had for parents with sick children. We had our own room with two twin beds in it. It was like a home away from home, so comforting and peaceful. My mom would go to the hospital with me every day and sit there and rock in that blue rocking chair, singing lullabies to Steven. She would make up silly songs and sing them to him, I would pretend I was sleeping sometimes and others I would just look at her and think to myself "when she dies, this is a moment I want to remember". I still do, and always will.

After that little hiccup, Steven maintained a normal blood sugar. I had to give him supplements in his formula and check his blood sugar every 3 hours for quite some time, I got into the routine of it ,but my sister moved out of my room cause she couldn't stand the baby crying and the alarm going off every 3 hours. It was funny, she was a teenager then, but now as a mommy, she knows what it was like for me. We continued to take Steven to the specialists until he was about 9 months old. He saw a metabolic specialist as well as an endocrinologist. I remember the specialists telling me about different disorders that Steven may have, but trying to remember what they were saying specifically now, I just can't do. It was so much to take in, and anyways, Steven was all better so it really didn't matter too much to me at that time. Things became somewhat normal again until my beautiful mom went to be with Jesus when Steven was almost 8 months old. I am so thankful that Steven had some time with his grandma, even though he doesn't remember her, I still can tell him the stories of her holding him, and singing to him, how much she loved him. I have a stuffed bunny that she gave him that Easter before she passed, he knows that his grandma Beri gave it to him, at least I have those memories of Steven and her together. That's what I miss the most I think, is that she is not here to be with him or to be with my nieces and nephews. The fact that my nieces will never know her, in a personal way just breaks my heart. My sister and brother make sure the girls know who their grandma was and always will keep her memory alive.

About a month after my mom passed, Steven was running a fever one day. It wasn't too high, it was in the hundreds, just a low grade fever. My dad was going somewhere that day so he left the house only to come right back and tell me to check Stevens temperature. He said he just "had a feeling". I checked it again, and it was 104. Once again we were on our way to the ER, I had no idea that this was just one of many trips to there. The doctors wanted to do a spinal tap and test for meningitis. Of course I said "yes, whatever you need to do to help him" I sat there while a STUDENT came to poke a needle about the size of a celery stick into my baby's spine. They didn't even sedate him.

I remember him screaming as I held him down, and then I saw blood. Blood everywhere, squirting out of my baby's body. The student didn't get the needle in the right spot and it caused blood to come flowing out of the needle as if someone turned on a hose! My dad
was so upset at them, he yelled and said to get a real doctor in there , he said "I don't want a student, I want a doctor, and a doctor who knows what they are doing!" I had to leave the room, I just couldn't handle it. Finally, a doctor did come and get the test done. We were just both so upset at this point, they still hadn't even given him anything to bring the fever down! It took us complaining to get them to give him something. His fever slowly went down, but they still admitted him for observation. He did fine that night, and the next morning when they couldn't find anything wrong, the doctor told us that Steven probably just an ear infection. They sent us home. I was glad, but looking back really naive, I was just glad that I didn't have any more problems with Steven, and that he was alright. Back to life as usual, a normal life. At least that's what I thought.

Introduced to seizures

Have you ever met someone that later you wished you had never met?, I am sure you have. Well, that's how I feel about seizures, I wish I had never even heard the word, or seen one. Steven was about 1yr old, maybe a little younger, I can't remember the exact age he was. It was a nice warm summer night, and I had just taken Steven out of the bathtub. He loved taking baths, and I love rubbing his smooth little chubby legs and arms with baby lotion. I loved how he used to smell after a bath, unlike the stinky teenager I have now! It was my favorite time to hold him and cuddle him, just to breathe him in. I had laid him on the bed and was getting ready to do my routine with him. As he was laying there and I noticed his tiny fist jerked a little. I just turned my head slightly thinking "hmm, that was weird". I just continued to do whatever it was I was doing when, he did it again, and again, and again. I picked him up and went in the living room where my older sister Dawn was, there along with my dad. I described to them what Steven was doing and they both started watching him with me. When he did it again, they agreed it was definitely strange, although very slight, it was noticeable. We all agreed that I should take him to the ER to see what was going on.

Once again, we were at the hospital, and it was the same hospital my mom passed away at so it was a little awkward being there again. I could still picture her in the ER, it was just strange. The ER doctor came in and I described to him what I saw Steven do. There is a blank space in my mind after that, but I do remember the doctor telling me that Steven had had a seizure. At that time, I had no idea about what tests to do or anything, I didn't know what and EEG was, so I just trusted the doctor and agreed to put Steven on a seizure medicine. I don't know how he knew for a fact that it was a seizure, because there were no tests done to confirm. I guess he just knew from the description I gave him. He told me to call his metabolic doctors at the other hospital and let them know what happened and sent us home. Like I said, it's all a blank for a while from there, I really can't remember how many seizures he had, or even his first real big seizure. I don't know why I can't remember, but I must have blocked it all out, or I have had so much to handle since then it is just buried in my brain somewhere gathering dust!

I did take Steven to the metabolic specialist who then sent him to see a neurologist. The neurologist put him on another medicine and that was pretty much it. In the meantime, Steven continued to thrive, although a little delayed, which I really wasn't aware of at that time, he seemed to be a normal healthy little boy, with exception to a few seizures. His seizures seemed to become worse and worse as he got older. The drop seizures started and I was so desperate for someone to "fix" him. Moving on, when Steven was about 4 yrs old he had been to so many different neurologists who just couldn't diagnose him. We had the diagnosis of epilepsy, but I wanted a name to what was wrong with him, not just "oh, he has seizures". He had been at the same hospital where he was admitted as a newborn, seeing the neurologists there since the seizures started, and I was feeling like they just didn't care. Every visit was like "here, try this medicine, increase this one, and decrease that one..Oh take him off of that one". I was so tired of it, there had to be someone better or more knowledgeable and caring to help my son. I was at work one day, and I was kind of spacing out, you know how work can do that you sometimes, and I thought of how my mom went to a hospital in Los Angeles for her medical treatment for her cirrhosis. I thought, maybe they would take Steven, they seemed very smart there and maybe I could get the answers that I needed. I asked my employer if it was ok for me to check on that hospital on the work computer and she agreed, she was such a sweet angel, I was blessed to have her as my employer. I looked up the hospital online, and I emailed a doctor. I really don't even know who the doctor was or what field he or she was in, I was just desperate. I asked the doctor if there was any way that I could bring my son to that hospital, I basically poured my heart out to that doctor, I told about Stevens story and how I just needed some help. I think it was the next day, I got an email back from that doctor. He or She said that there was a long waiting list to get into the pediatric neurology department, but, she somehow got me an appointment and referred me to the doctor that would be taking care of Steven for the next 11 years. I was a miracle, I think that God lead me to that doctor who I emailed.

Lennox Gastaut Syndrome

The day came for us to take Steven to the new hospital. I was so excited, at that time, I was still so full of hope and thought that my son could be cured, I feel like I was so clueless back then. We waited in the waiting room and finally we were called into the smaller patient room. It was a nice hospital, lots of kids with different disabilities, unlike what I had ever seen before. The patient room was on the left side, I still remember what room it was, I sat in a rocking chair holding Steven. We must have waited over an hour for the doctor to come in, which was unusual because we have never had to wait that long in the 11 years since then. When the doctor came in, she looked so sweet. She was a small petite woman, and she looked like she was only about 30. She was very nice and friendly, she even laughed, and I hadn't ever laughed with any other doctors before. All of the other doctors were so serious and seemed like they wanted to just get rid of us. I will call her Dr. W, she said that she had looked over his history, and she wanted to do some blood work, and an EEG. I was so excited to be having some tests done on Steven!! She told us to come back for a follow-up visit after the results were in. I was just so happy that someone finally cared and looked forward to the results, but at the next visit my life changed forever.

Again ,I still remember what room we were in for the follow up visit. Dr. W sat down with me and my dad and she explained that Steven had something called Lennox Gastaut Syndrome. I was terrified, it sounded so bad. I immediately asked her "Is he going to die?" I can't believe that was my first question, but I think that was my biggest fear. She assured me that he want going to die, but explained to me a little bit about Lennox Gastaut Syndrome. I think she took him off of one of his medicines and added another at that time, I was just hopeful that she could cure him, even though she said there is no cure for LGS, I still wanted to prove the disease wrong. I had my answer, my diagnosis, but it still didn't get me anywhere like I thought it would. Back then, I didn't have internet or even own a computer so I had to go to the library and try to research. I couldn't find much out about LGS, so I just lived with it, hoping and praying that one of these medicines would work.

Life went on, Steven had seizures. He had the drop seizures so bad that he had to get a helmet, the same kind that I had seen on the kids in elementary school. I hated that he had to wear it, and I didn't make him wear it like I should have, especially not in public. I learned my lesson one night when my cousin came running out of the bathroom yelling "he had a seizure, he is bleeding". I was terrified. I went running into the bathroom and there was blood everywhere. I don't think I had seen that much blood in my life. Steven had a drop seizure and hit his head on the toilet. We rushed him to the ER for his first, of many, sets of stitches. Let me explain what a drop seizure is for those who don't know. I am not very good at describing the different seizure types, but what it looks like is this: He would be sitting at a table and his head would just drop, and I don't mean slowly, it was like someone hit him on the head with a baseball bat and his head went flying forward. If he was in a standing position, he would drop head first to the ground, again, like someone hit him so hard to force him down. These were one of the worst seizures types that Steven had. I eventually had to give in and keep him in the helmet a little more than I wanted to, but it was for his own safety.

Time for School

That same year as the LGS diagnosis, Steven was to start preschool. I was so excited for him to go to school. A meeting was set up with some school district staff and I was told that from what they knew and observed of Steven that he would have to be in special education. I was thinking "alright, so its special education, please don't tell me it's that school by my elementary school, please, please, not that". One of the staff told me what school he would be going to, it was that special school, the one that I had never ever expected my child to go to. I wanted to cry, I had to hold back tears forming in my eyes. I wanted to scream at them and tell them that I refuse for him to go there. I asked them "well, if he has to go there, he will be able to go to a (normal) school next year, right?". They told me that it was a possibility, and that this was the proper placement for him at this time. I think that's one of the first times that reality finally set in, that Steven was different, and that life was going to be different. Ironic thing, is that now at this time in my life, I would give anything for Steven to be at that same school.

Steven finished his preschool year, and we, meaning my dad, sister, me and Steven, decided to try to move to another state to see if it would be financially better for us. We moved to Bullhead City, AZ. It was a big difference from Southern California. It was HOT, but we loved it. We rented a little mobile home, and me and my sister both obtained jobs. I worked at a casino and she worked at the mall. I was hoping that life would be better for all of us, including Steven and the seizures. We had to drive to Phoenix to see a specialist for his seizures, it was about a 4 hour drive, I don't remember our visit, or even the doctors name, at that time, the seizures weren't that bad and it wasn't a really big deal to me. We didn't stay there long, we missed our family in CA and ended up moving back to CA for a while, only to move back to Bullhead City a few years later to give it another try. It was at that time Steven had to start kindergarten. A meeting was held, oh how I dreaded that meeting, I didn't want to hear yet again that he would have to be in special education. At this meeting, I actually told the staff that Steven was in special education in his preschool, and was amazed at what I heard next. The man who was in charge told me that Steven was way to functional to be in the special education class. He said that it would only hurt him to be put there, that he would not thrive from his peers in that class being that most of them were non verbal. He said Steven should be in a normal kindergarten class. I was elated to hear this. I felt as if I proved all those people wrong in CA, I left with the biggest smile on my face, I knew that Steven wasn't as bad as they thought he was. Now at this time, for some reason, he wasn't having the drop seizures very often, and of course, I didn't make him wear his helmet, I didn't feel there was a need for one. His kindergarten year was great, he sang songs in class, colored picture, well more like scribbled pictures, and he just loved it. We even went on a field trip to the fire station. The teacher was wonderful, one of the most patient women I have even known. She did end up having trouble with Steven, and the school started to see it as well. They staff tried to make it comfortable for Steven, they even started sending the fifth graders in to help with Steven during the day. One time, I went to pick him up from school and I was told that he went to the bathroom and came out naked, poor teacher looked so tired out, I felt bad for her, but I couldn't help but laugh. It was a good year, but unfortunately we decided it was time for us to move back to California, Bullhead City just wasn't where we wanted to be. Before we left, Steven and I went to the store and bought his teacher a beta fish in a vase with a plant in it, to thank her. Steven was so excited to give her that fish.

Grand Mal

We were back in California again. With little money and nowhere to go My Aunt and Uncle were kind enough to let me, my dad and Steven stay at their house. The three of us shared a small room, and it was hard, but at least we had somewhere to call home. My sister decided to go to my grandma's house and live with her, it was hard for me because my sister was my best friend, and she was my support, my strength. I don't think she knew how much I needed her, and how much of a help she was to me, and I don't think I ever told her back then because she was still so young, I didn't want to put a burden on her or make her feel guilty. I missed her a lot, but I still got to see her since she was only about 30 minutes away. I was just hard since losing my mom to not live with my sister, or my brother. My brother had moved in with our aunt and uncle before we even moved to Arizona. I just didn't like having our family be apart. Being back in California was nice, the rest of my family was here, and I loved the weather and the Beach. This time I hoped for things to be different financially and that I could work and that Stevens seizures would be under control. Unfortunately, I was too hard to work and take care of Steven, I had no idea that he was about to have the worst seizure he had ever had. My dad and I were getting out of the car one day, and my dad was carrying Steven in my arms into the house. I noticed that he just was limp. I yelled to my dad "Something's wrong", Steven was barely breathing, his lips were starting to turn blue. My dad said to call an ambulance, but I told him that we were getting in the car and going to the hospital ourselves. I couldn't wait for an ambulance. My dad was driving as fast as he could, he was even running red lights. I was in the backseat, crying and screaming for him to wake up. He was non- responsive, his face was blue and he still wasn't breathing. I thought he was gone. I can still feel that emotion and fear that I felt in the car that day, I remember it so clearly. On the way, we saw and Police car driving by, my dad flagged the police car down and we pulled over. The police car turned around and I got Steven out of the car. The officer called an ambulance immediately. As soon as I got Steven out of the car, he came out of the seizure, he threw up everywhere and took the biggest deep breath. I was so happy to hear that deep breath, I didn't even care that I was covered in vomit, I was just happy that he was still with me. We ended up going to the hospital in the ambulance, and I was told that he had a Grand Mal seizure (also known as a Tonic Clonic). Once again, just when I thought I knew it all, and that he was under control, another slap in the face. All I knew was that I never wanted to see another one of those again. Looking back, it's funny now because Steven had just ate a candy bar with coconut and almonds right before the Grand Mal. To this day we still don't give him that particular candy bar, I guess back then we were trying to blame something for the seizures, but I know for sure now that it wasn't that candy bar.

A new kind of school for Steven

Steven started school again back in California. He was put into a regular school, but in the special education classroom. I was ok with it, because I know how hard it was for his kindergarten teacher the previous year. He loved his new teacher, and his new friends, but unfortunately, he didn't get to stay there for very long. I think it was about 6 months into the school year and I was called in for a meeting. It was decided that Steven needed to be in the county class for the severely disabled children. I was very upset, I even cried afterward. You form a bond with the teachers, and the staff in the classrooms, I didn't want to have to start over, they were like family to us, and he had to be put in an even more disabled class? This whole school thing was upsetting, but little did I know that I was about to meet the best teacher in the whole world, and I mean it, she is something special. We said our goodbyes at his school, and I made an appointment with the new teacher to go meet her before I send Steven to her class. I always like to meet the teachers and see the classrooms before I send him, I want to get a feel of the environment, and the teacher. When I went to see the class, it was a modular trailer in the back of an elementary school, I wasn't impressed. The teacher opened the door and I just knew that it wasn't going to work. This teacher was older than his last teacher, how was she supposed to keep up with Steven? She was very nice, but she was to the point and didn't try to sugar coat anything. I left the school, and I was crying. I never told her this, because I was so wrong in my first impression. I will call her Mrs. P.. Steven loved her, he loved the teachers' aides in the class, Mrs. C and Mr. G. This teacher was so caring, so loving. She actually cared about the kids in her class and the parents as well. I will jump ahead just a bit and then get back to my story, but Steven stayed in her class for 4 years. The best years Steven ever had in school. Poor Mrs. P even cried one time when Steven had a drop seizure and bumped his head on the chalkboard and cut it open, he had to get stitches. She felt so bad, but it wasn't her fault. At that time, the district wouldn't give me a one on one aide for Steven and she only had 2 others to help in a classroom of 10 kids. She was amazing though. The teacher would have pot lucks in the class for us parents, always lots of good food. She even planned a "moms night out" for us parents to just get a break once a month. We would all get together and go have dinner and just talk for a few hours. I was more than just a bunch of moms getting together, it was a support group as well. I wouldn't be where I am now if it weren't for those special moms nights out.

A new treatment, the Ketogenic diet

So, we were back in CA and Steven was in a new school, where I finally felt safe and we were going back to the hospital in Los Angeles. At one of the appointments Dr. W asked us if we wanted to try the Ketogenic diet on Steven. I had heard of it, even seen a movie about it, so I was very optimistic about it, and of course I would try anything that would help my son. She informed me that Steven would need to stay overnight in the hospital and that I would need to attend a class on the ketogenic diet. I was excited to learn something new that could help Steven, so it was not a problem for me, and back then, I actually liked overnight stays in the hospital, I don't know why, maybe it was just being away from where were living for a while, but I didn't mind. After attending the class, it actually was just Stevens nutritionist and myself, I went and bought all the necessary things that I would need for the diet. Small bowls with lids, I got colored ones so I could plan and prepare his meals ahead of time, I would use a certain color for breakfast, lunch, dinner and snacks. I was ready. I was ready for the seizures to be gone, ready for this diet to cure him. The day we checked into the hospital, I was eagerly anticipating what was to come. I was a little disappointed that the room we were in was a shared room, but I will get to that in a minute, everything happens for a reason. They started the diet, most kids have to fast before starting but because of Stevens previous blood sugar difficulties, and he couldn't fast, so they did a modified version of the diet. I remember that they started him on a heavy cream, he drank it very easily as he has always been such a good eater. That night, I noticed something that I had seen before, something a very long time ago, he was lethargic, meaning, weak and not really alert. I called the nurse in and his blood sugar dropped to 20. They immediately gave him some orange juice to get his sugar up, and we had to stop the diet for that night. We started again the next morning, again with another modified plan and this time he was able to tolerate it. I learned how to measure out all of his food, every bite he took had to be measured and consumed. Even the residue on the bowl had to be scraped and eaten. At the time, I thought it would be a piece of cake, no problem, I could do this at home. It actually wasn't that hard once I had the hang of it. They released him after 2 nights and we headed back to our little room at my uncles house. I prepared his breakfast, lunch, snacks and dinner every couple of days. It took me about an hour and a half to make food for a few days in advance. I would weigh everything, and separate it all into its little color coded bowls and plates and store it in the refrigerator. At first, I had it down, I was good at it and I enjoyed preparing the food and learning new recipes that I could make for him. Steven loved all of the food, and I was amazed at the fact that he would drink the heavy cream and even eat chunks of butter plain, yes, my child is a very good eater! After about 3 months of the diet, I just couldn't handle it anymore. I wasn't helping his seizures much, although he did go 8 days seizure free which was the longest he had ever went since the seizures started. I just wasn't getting my "cure" fast enough and I was tired, so tired of waiting and putting in all the time and effort to make the food and weigh it, I had just had enough. I called the nurse who worked with us for the keto diet and told her I had to stop. She asked me if I was sure and I definitely was sure. Looking back now, it really wasn't the diet, it was just everything that was going on in my life at the time, between the seizures, and where I was living, plus the cost of the diet while on a very small income, it just all added up and I think it was just too much for me to take on at that time in my life. So the diet was done, not a success, but I only gave it 3 months and it can take up to 2 years to see results. So much for that "cure", I almost forgot to mention something that happened on that visit. I said things happen for a reason, and there was a reason we were in a shared room. In this room, there was a young girl, she was 15. I remember when they brought her in, it was late at night, I could hear her parents saying stuff like "hold her up" and "move her legs". I figured that she probably couldn't walk, but I didn't know what was wrong with her. It was sometime during the next morning, I overheard them talking about her having seizures. I tried not to be nosey, but I couldn't help it, I was curious. I started talking to my dad about Stevens seizures pretty loud so that they could overhear me and maybe they would initiate a conversation. They did and I found out that the girl couldn't walk, she could barely even talk, couldn't use the toilet or even feed herself. I learned that she was not always that way. She used to be able to run, and do things that a little girl should do. I didn't ask if she ever talked better. They said that she had just regressed over the years. They told me that she had LGS. I think my mouth probably fell open, but I wanted to cry and say "NO". Was this what I was to expect to happen to Steven. I just tried to be sympathetic, and not selfish, but I couldn't help the selfishness, I didn't want my boy to be like that, I wanted him to get better. They added that they had put her on a medication that they got from Canada, I will call it Med "O". It supposedly worked very well on her and was greatly reducing her seizures. I wrote the name down, but I knew I couldn't afford to get a medication from Canada and pay with cash, another ironic thing in this journey, this medicine would be the one later in his life that would help him the most.

Vagal Nerve Stimulator

Still living at my uncles house, I think Steven was about 7 or 8 years old. Dr. W put Steven on that medicine from Canada "O". I was so excited to give it a try since I had heard about it from the people in the hospital. He was on it for about a month, and unfortunately it didn't help him, and was too expensive to get from out of the country, we stopped it and continued on as best as we could. Our next option was the Vagal Nerve Stimulator. Now, Steven had never had a surgery, and at that time I was much scarred. I mean, he had had MRI's under sedation before, but never been in surgery, this was something new and I was unfamiliar with it all. At this time, Stevens seizures were getting worse, none of the medications were working to control the seizures, and the drop seizures were just unbearable. Steven had at least 20 seizures daily. I felt that by getting the VNS, it would help him, and possibly stop the seizures. I met with the neurosurgeon at the hospital in Los Angeles. I was very leery of him at first, he wasn't like Dr. W, who laughed and was very friendly. This guy was absolutely straightforward and to the point. I will tell you more about this neurosurgeon later, I learned that my first impressions of people were way off. He told us the risks, and the benefits and the fact that it may not even help at all. I had to try it, just like everything else, I had to do it. What if I didn't do a procedure that could help Steven? Anything that would even have a chance to help him, I would try. I finally had internet so I was able to research the VNS and I was very excited, once again and hopeful. Surgery was scheduled within 2 weeks of our meeting. Surgery day came, we checked him in and they rolled him on the journey into surgery. He was so little back then, I felt so helpless, and I couldn't help but cry. I had no idea what was to come in the future and that this surgery was like plucking a splinter out of a finger, but in that moment, I was so heartbroken that he had to go thru this. The surgery took about an hour, and Steven was in recovery for about 2 hours. The VNS was not turned on at the time of surgery, that would be scheduled for about a week later. He had a cut on his neck, held together with some dissolvable stitches and some type of medical tape. He also had a cut on the crease of his armpit, also held together by dissolvable stitches and tape. The cuts weren't as bad as I thought they would be, but the VNS implant itself looked so big inside his little skinny chest. It was about the size of a silver dollar. Steven didn't complain of any pain and we went home that same day. I think the hardest part of that whole recovery was trying to keep the tape on Stevens neck, of course it was ripped off the very next day. He hates anything on his body that isn't supposed to be there. When the VNS was finally turned on, it was on a very low setting. You see, with the VNS the doctor has a little "wand" type thing that is placed on the site where the device is in his chest and hooked up to a computer. The "wand" is placed on the chest over the VNS, the computer then is able to read all the information related to Stevens device. The neurologist can set the frequency that it "goes off", like it would go off every 30 seconds then be off for 30 for example. They could also set the power of the stimulator. It's hard to explain, but it's like an electrical current, they can set the voltage to it. They gave me 2 high powered magnets to use with the VNS after surgery as well. These magnets are used when he would go into a seizure, or before a seizure if you could catch it. I would swipe the magnet on the implant and it would immediately activate the device sending the electrical impulse to his brain to try to stop the seizure. Unfortunately, the VNS didn't help Steven at that time, it was another let down, and by then I was getting pretty used to being let down. I wouldn't say I was losing hope, but I was realizing more and more of what a powerful monster I was dealing with in LGS.

Thankful for some changes

Backing up a little, remember how I was talking about my sons teacher and how we would have moms night out? How I said that changed my life? Well, now comes the part where I can explain that to you. We were out at a restaurant, I think it was our 2nod or 3rd moms night. One of the other moms mentioned to me that she got paid to take care of her son who was autistic. I had never heard of anything like that, I was just on welfare and received Stevens social security, I didn't know there were any other programs that could help financially. She gave me all of the information, and I called the next day and signed up for Steven. I was hoping to get this help, as I couldn't work, I had to put all of my time into taking care of Steven. It took about 2 weeks and I got a phone call that a case worker would be out to my house to evaluate Steven. I was so excited, this could change our lives. It was a couple of weeks later when the case worker came to my house. When he showed up, I was a little embarrassed at where I was living, but at this time we had the house to ourselves, as my uncle had moved to another home and let us continue paying the rent there. The house had little furniture and kind of smelled bad, but hey, it was a roof over our heads. Of course later, I found that the case worker had mentioned that in his notes. He asked me all kinds of questions, if I bathed Steven and how long it took, if I brushed his teeth, helped with toileting, stuff like that. He didn't pay too much attention to Steven, but I really didn't think that mattered much because it was about what I do to care for Steven. The man left and I eagerly waited for a response to his evaluation in the mail. It was a couple of months later and I received a letter stating that Steven was not approved, I was heartbroken, and I just started crying. They said that epilepsy was not a disabling condition and for that reason he was not approved for the service. My dad told me "Georgia, you have to fight, appeal it…you deserve this for Steven". He was right, and I appealed. It was another few months and it was time for my day in court. I was to show up before a mediator, or a judge, with Steven and plead my case to him. Just my luck, Steven was put on a drug, I will call it drug D, and he had a toxic reaction and was in the hospital for a week. I went the appeal, without Steven, and I explained why he was not there. The judge continued the hearing, and it seemed like he was on my side. The case workers point as well as the whole program was that Epilepsy was not considered a disabling condition and that is why Steven was denied. Well, just to let you know, I was prepared. I had letters from his teacher, a psychological evaluation report, letters from everyone I knew, including his doctors stating that Steven was not mentally able to care for himself and needed my protective supervision in order to remain in his home. The judge decided that he needed to see Steven for himself, so a date was scheduled and he came to our home. I almost want to laugh now, because it was so obvious that we were entitled to this help. The judge came to my house about a month later. When he arrived, he only wanted to talk to Steven, not me. He asked Steven where the store was and Steven pointed to outside. The judge told Steven to show him how he goes to the store, and Steven walked toward the front door. I got up and proceeded to stop him, but the judge stopped me and said that he wanted to see where Steven would go. Steven opened the front door and went to the porch where he had a play kitchen. Steven said "the store is here ". The judge clearly could see that Steven needed help, and you better believe, a month later, I received my approval letter and was awarded the highest amount of hours and a whole years worth of back pay. I again cried, and thanked God. I could finally move, and have a home of my own, and not worry about money, get off of welfare. I was truly thankful that I could have my life back.

As soon as I received my check, we moved to a new town about 60 miles from where we were lived for so long. My grandpa lived here, so it was nice to have some family close by. We rented a beautiful home, three bedrooms, and two baths only 2 years old. I loved that house, I finally felt like I was home which had been a feeling I hadn't felt in a very long time. Steven loved his huge room, he loved just simply having his own room. I decorated it in the colors of his favorite movie character, and had all the stuffed animals to go along with it. We had our 2 cats, Fluffy and Elvis and ended up getting 2 dogs, Barney and Fred. They were both yellow lab mixes, brothers. Steven liked the dogs and cats from a distance, but he didn't really care to play with them or pet them.

Regression

Regression. A word that I very much dislike. I first noticed Steven regressing when it was again time for a new school. It really wasn't that bad of a transition since Mrs. P from his old school had moved out of state, so there weren't all the emotions this time. Steven started the 4th grade out here. He again was in the special ed class, but by this time, I knew that's where he needed to be and I wasn't going to even try to place him in a regular class. The teacher was very nice, not Mrs. P, but a very nice lady. There were 2 teachers aides in the class and Steven ended up really loving both of them. At the time he started school that year, Steven could spell over 100 words, and I'm not talking just the 3 letter words, he could spell words like "alligator". He would tell me what he learned in class, not very detailed but I would know if he heard a certain book, or sang a song. He wasn't functioning like a normal child his age, but he was doing pretty well. I can't say for sure where everything started going downhill, but it seems like when we moved, the old Steven stayed behind. He slowly started forgetting how to spell words, and spelling was (and still is) his strong point. He wouldn't tell me what he did in class anymore, I could see he was regressing. His seizures were worse and more frequent. He was finally wearing his helmet full time because the drop seizures were the worst. He would go to school and sleep most of the time, but, luckily the school and the teachers were so patient and sympathetic towards him, he was allowed to sleep as he needed. The school year went on and the seizures continued. I think this was a point in our lives where we were just in limbo. We had tried most of the seizures medications on Steven with no success, tried the Keto diet as well as the Modified Atkins diet and the Low Gylcemic Index treatment (all similar to the keto diet, just easier). Nothing was going to make these seizures leave my son. I prayed like no other mother could pray, I just wanted him to be alright. Skipping ahead, while I am on the subject, regression is one of the hardest parts of LGS. It seems like every time I think Steven is learning something, it gets taken away. I can remember when he was little, he would sing his ABC's, and sing songs. I miss his sweet little singing voice, as he doesn't sing anymore. He can still tell you most of his ABC's, but he cannot sing them and forgets a letter here and there. He doesn't really have long conversations anymore, although he will still talk, actually he never stops talking, but it's mostly repetitive. Regression is hard to accept, but it's just another part of LGS that I hate.

Corpus Callosotomy, aka..Brain surgery

 Over the years I was told about something called SUDEP (sudden unexpected death in epilepsy). I was surprised that I wasn't aware of it for so long, I actually learned about it on the internet, as I was a pro at looking up anything and everything by then. SUDEP is similar to SIDS (sudden infant death syndrome) the child or adult will just be found dead. They suspect it's a seizure during sleep, but there is no explanation for the deaths. They just die. This was my biggest fear, losing my son. To this day he sleeps right beside me because of my fear of SUDEP. I brought this up because it plays a very important role in my next decision. A decision that no parent should ever have to make. I was at a drugstore getting a prescription for Steven one night, it must have been at least 6 pm. Stevens neurologist called me for something, I think it was for lab results. Anyways, she asked me if I had ever thought of doing the corpus colostomy on Steven. I was shocked, because I brought up the option for surgery for Steven years ago and she had told me that he was not a candidate because his seizures were not localized (in one particular part of his brain). I told her that I was definitely interested, she told me to look it up on the internet and really think about it and if I was ready, to call her and she would send the referral to the neurosurgeon. As soon as I got home, I was looking up everything I could about corpus colostomy. What this procedure is, is the surgeon split's the two hemispheres of the brain so that the seizure activity cannot cross from one side to another, therefore, stopping the drop seizures. The surgery was sometimes done all at one time, meaning cutting the entire corpus callosum in one procedure, completely separating the two hemispheres. Other surgeons opt to do it in two parts. First cutting the front 2/3rds and if not successful, going in and cutting the remaining part about a year later. This was so scary to me. Of course I wanted to do it, if it was an option and had even a tiny chance of helping, I was ready. This was brain surgery though. I called the neurologist and told her to get me the referral, I had to do this before I changed my mind.

Sitting in the neurosurgeons office, the same guy that did Stevens VNS, I think I was just in a different world. I could barely believe that I was there again, and this time to put my son thru brain surgery. I had to sign the consent then and there, I knew that once that consent was signed a surgery date wouldn't be too far away. I was ready, well, I thought I was. Walking into Dr. M's (that's what I will refer to him as) office, I thought I knew exactly what to expect, after all, I knew it all from the internet. This time Dr. M was still very serious and to the point, but he was more caring, and kind. He explained the whole procedure, just as he did before the VNS. He told me that the whole neurology team had to agree that Steven needed this surgery to even think about doing it. He said that the risk of SUDEP was greater than the risks of the surgery. That's all I needed to hear. I signed the papers. Surgery was scheduled a few weeks later. I remember leaving the hospital that day and crying, yet I was numb, it was such a mix of emotions. It was almost unbelievable that I had to consent for my son to have brain surgery. About a month before the surgery date, I had second thoughts. There was a new medicine that had just been approved by the FDA and I wanted to try it before going into surgery. It was a hard decision, because I had already prepared myself, but I called and canceled his surgery date, but still left the option open by leaving all the approvals just on hold for a while. Steven started the new medicine (I will call it medicine B), with no luck, no change. I rescheduled the surgery and within a month we in the hospital. Steven was to stay the night prior to surgery in the hospital. We checked in and we ended up waiting 8 hours to be admitted into a room. While we were waiting, my dad told me that he thought it was a sign that we weren't supposed to have the surgery done. We almost left, but I went outside and prayed that we would get in soon, and when I came back in, the nurse said his room was ready. It was a hard night, I tried not to think about what tomorrow would bring. I think I was kind of in shock that this was actually happening. I can't really explain how I felt, it was as if I was out of my body or something. I just cuddled my boy all that night and held him a little tighter, just in case it would be my last time. The next morning, they took him down to pre op. We waited about 2 hours before he went into the OR. I can still see the surgeon standing at the door of the OR telling me that it would be alright. Dr. M even gave me a hug. They wheeled Steven into surgery and my dad and I burst into tears. It was as if I had been holding it in and as soon as Steven went it, I let it out, and I was back in my body and feeling every emotion possible. We went straight to the chapel and got on our knees and begged God to spare him, to bring him back to us, to keep him safe. I prayed and cried like I never have in my life. We brought ourselves to be able to stop crying and went to the waiting room. At this hospital it is very nice how the whole operating procedure works. They give you a pager first of all so if you are eating or outside they can page you if you are needed. Also, the nurse in the OR calls down to the waiting room and the attendant gives you the phone. The nurse notifies you when the surgery has started, when it's in the middle, and when they are closing him up. It's nice to know the progress of the surgery instead of not hearing anything for several hours. I do know that every time that phone rang I was on pins and needles, and when it was for me, my heart must have been beating out of my chest. The surgery took about 5 hours (it was supposed to take 7). As soon as Steven was in recovery, they called down to the waiting room so that I could go up and be with him. I practically ran down the halls, up the elevator and into recovery. Stevens face was swollen, he had a white gauze like head wrap around his whole head. He had a tube coming out of his neck and IV's in his arms. He really didn't wake up for me, but he did open his eyes and said something, then went back to sleep. I was just so great full that he did open his eyes and he recognized me. I knew he was my same boy, but I was still fearful because he had just got out of surgery. They soon moved him to the PICU. My sister and her husband were able to come in and see him, and of course Steven woke up for his aunt Danna (Danielle). She had him talking a little bit and I think she was feeding him ice chips. She realized that he was warm and told the nurse. He had a pretty high fever, but I guess that is normal, so she gave him something for it and we basically all called it a night. I don't think I slept very well that night, but I know I slept as I was so tired from the whole day. They allowed both my dad and myself stay in the room with Steven, we had to share a blue fold out chair, but at least we got to be with him. Our time in the hospital was about 4 days, and Steven seemed to be just fine. He did have problems having a bowel movement, but they discharged him with instructions for me to use at home. I was not prepared for what was to come. The drive home was hectic. I was so afraid to have his head move by a bump in the road, or one of the staples to get snagged somehow. He had 27 staples by the way, it was a cut across the front top of his head. Getting home was nice, but I was on my own now, no nurses in case of an emergency. I got Steven in bed, I made a barrier on the wall with a small thin foam mattress so that his head wouldn't hit it. He just slept. He ate a little, and then he slept. Then he would throw up, and throw up some more. He just couldn't hold down any food. Besides that, Steven couldn't walk, and barely could talk. He could only say maybe one word and the rest was mumbles. I was not told this would happen. Was he going to stay like this forever? I ended up taking him to the emergency room for the vomiting. They realized that his body cannot tolerate medicine "D" which I had told them before that he had a toxic reaction to it, but they insisted on giving it to him as they do with all patients having that surgery. As soon as we took him off of medicine "D", he started to hold down food. I would say that it took a good month or 2 before he was somewhat back to normal. He went 48 days without a seizure, and then one day, my heart dropped when I saw a grand mal and then a drop seizure. The surgery didn't work, which meant, we would have to do this all over again. The seizures just got worse, probably worse than before and I dreaded having to go to Dr. "M"s office again.

Make a Wish

During the time we were waiting for Steven to recover and heal from the Corpus Callosotomy, I decided to apply to a foundation that grants wishes for children with chronic or terminal illnesses. I figured that he was old enough to decide what his wish would be and we waited. It was a few weeks and we got a call to come in for an appointment with the wish team to discuss Stevens wish. I was so happy for Steven, he needed this, and he needed some fun for once, something that HE wanted to do. At the meeting he really wasn't talking much for some reason, but we all decided that he would go swim with the dolphins I didn't know where they would be sending us to, although I have to admit I was hoping for Hawaii. We later learned that we were going to a dolphin facility in Key Largo Florida. This place specializes in disabled children, each child has their own 2 dolphins and a therapist during the weeklong visit to the facility. We were all so excited. The wish team came to our home and threw a party as a "have fun Steven"day. They brought Stevens favorite foods, salad, and chicken nuggets. The cake they brought was absolutely beautiful, it was like an ocean, with dolphins on the top of it, it said "have fun Steven". There were even huge dolphin balloons and presents for Steven to take on his trip. The wish team gave me a folder with all the information about the flights and the limo that would be picking us up, really? A limo? It was only the beginning. They also gave a very nice check to cash and spend on the trip on whatever Steven wanted. I couldn't help but cry, this was just so amazing. The trip would be in 4 days, and we thanked the ladies and prepared for our trip. It would be Stevens first time on an airplane, I was so excited for him and besides, I love airplanes. My dad wasn't too happy to be up in the air, he hates flying. Steven laughed when the plane took off, and for the most part of the first half, it was pretty miserable. We had to fly from CA to Dallas and then from Dallas to Miami. Steven didn't like sitting in the plane for all of the hours. He was cussing, hitting, kicking the passenger in front of us, it was a nightmare. The second part of the flight wasn't too bad, from Dallas to Miami, because Steven took his medications and it pretty much knocked him out. We arrived in Miami about 12 am. The wish foundation paid for a very nice SUV rental and we proceeded to the Keys. I was amazed at the humidity in Florida, we don't have humidity here in CA. It seemed like we were driving forever down the highway, there was ocean on both sides of the road, even though it was dark, it was still a sight. Luckily I had GPS on my phone so we didn't get lost, but when we got to the hotel, I was in shock. It was beautiful and our room was on the second floor with a balcony that overlooked the turquoise ocean. The beds had big fluffy pillows and nice cozy comforters. It was a little hard to fall asleep that night due to the 3 hour time difference, but we all managed. The next morning, we had to be at the dolphin facility by 9 am. I woke Steven up and showed him the ocean, he just had a big smile and said he wanted to go swimming. I told him we were going to see the dolphins and he was ready to go. The facility was only about 5 minutes from the hotel, and very easy to find. When we arrived, there was a sign with the names of all the kids who were attending that week, welcoming them. We went up an elevator which took us to the lobby area. There were fish aquariums, and all sorts of info on dolphins, and a little gift shop. All of us parents and kids attend a welcome orientation and then it was off to the class with the therapist. Now each kid was assigned his or her own therapist, and they would work in a classroom making fun projects and then the therapist and the family would head down to the dolphins. Each child had his or her own 2 dolphins, Stevens dolphins were named Bella and Fiji. As far as the classroom part, Steven tried his best, but remembers, we are from CA, and the 3 hour difference really didn't agree with Steven as it would have only been 6 am in CA. He was very sleepy, but he still managed to make some pretty neat souvenirs to take home with him. When it was time to go down to swim with the dolphins, he suddenly woke up. He was fitted into a wetsuit and it was time to swim. The therapist jumped into the water first, and then Steven followed, wearing his life jacket The water was pretty cold, as it was in March, but it didn't seem to bother Steven much. At first he was more interested in swimming than the dolphins. As soon as Steven started to interact with Bella and Fiji, he was in love. He would hold their fins as they swam in the water and the smile on Stevens face was unforgettable. They had the dolphins do so many different things with Steven, they would splash him, bring him toys and jump through hoops for him while he was holding the hoop. Now these dolphins are special, they are in their own ocean water in a cove that is blocked off. They are not just dolphins that put on tricks and shows, they are for the kids. They are treated very well and not fed each time they do a trick. The dolphins do this on their own. It was just truly amazing. I think Stevens favorite part of the day was getting to go to the pool at the hotel. The pool had a huge waterfall that came over the top of a cave type thing, it's hard to explain ,but he loved it. We didn't get to stay long because what I didn't realize about Florida is that it rains quite a bit, and we got rained on quite a bit. We tried to go look around at different things in the Keys, it was so beautiful, I could have stayed there forever. Steven was a little bored though, I think it's a place more for adults. The third day we were there, after our session with the dolphins we went to a sea life place. Stevens favorite part was, well, sleeping. We couldn't keep him awake for anything. The only thing that he really saw was a sea lion show with a sea lion called Wilbur, he still talks about it to this day. Day 4, we had a family barbeque at the dolphin facility, it was a nice time to talk to other parents and the staff, then afterward we decided to drive back to Miami and go to the football stadium. The Dolphins are Stevens favorite football team, thanks to his aunt Danielle. I ended up getting us lost, as my phone wasn't charged to use the GPS, so I thought I could read a map. Ya, right. I took us to a pretty scary part of Miami, and my dad kept telling me that we were going the wrong way, but I insisted that the map was right, or that I was right. There were men coming up to the cars selling already peeled oranges, I have never seen anything like it. I finally realized that I was reading the map upside down, and we quickly found our way. I had to call my sister and tell her we were going to the Dolphins stadium, I was so excited to share it with her, even though she couldn't be with us, it was special. Once at the stadium, the lady at the entrance booth wasn't going to let us in, as there was a baseball game that night. I told her that we were from CA and my son was on his wish trip. I practically begged, and she finally agreed that we could only go to the gift shop and she had to hold my license, that was fine with me. I took lots of pictures with Steven in front of the stadium, and in front of the gift shop I bought him a Dolphins t shirt, which was so exciting to actually buy it from the place where the dolphins play football. It was a great day. The final day at the dolphin facility was emotional. To start the day off, Steven had a grand mal seizure at the hotel and we almost had to call the ambulance. Luckily he came out of it, but he was not going to be able to swim with HIS dolphins on that final day. He still says they were HIS dolphins!! It was also the day that I was supposed to swim with the dolphins I regret not going in, you see, I am afraid of fish, I know, it's so stupid but that is my phobia. I just couldn't go in that water with the little fishes that swam in the ocean water, they freaked me out. Besides, we had to leave there immediately and go to the airport for the long flight home and I didn't want to be full of saltwater for such a long trip. We said our goodbyes, and of course I cried, it was hard to leave an experience like that, I am still hoping that someday we can return there. We made it to the airport and made the long flight home, again, Steven acting up. The limo was waiting at the airport for us, and we had a nice drive home.

Corpus Callosotomy, part 2

Life was back to reality once again. Wish trip was over and it was time for doctors appointments, behavior issues, just my same old life. We took Steven to see Dr. W and within a month, we had seen the neurosurgeon, Dr. M and were preparing for another brain surgery, to finish the corpus colostomy. This surgery was a little more risky. The biggest risk was that Steven would never talk again. I guess most children who have this done are non verbal, so this was a big deal with Steven, as he never stops talking. It was another one of those decisions that was so hard to make but I knew that I had to do it. Of course I signed the consent papers, and all of the other stuff needed before surgery. I made little videos with Steven talking just in case I would never get the chance to hear his voice, it was so bittersweet to look at those videos because I had faith that he would be alright but at the same time I still knew the risks. I can recall the night before, I just prayed, my uncle came over as I was praying with a woman on the internet and he joined us. My uncle didn't agree that I should do the surgery on Steven It was so hard for me to have anyone tell me not to do it, because unless they are in my shoes, they have no idea what it's like to see your son being hurt every day by these seizures. People don't know how many times I have cried because I just felt like I couldn't do it anymore. This upset me that night because I had already prepared myself and I was at peace with my decision. I didn't need any negativity. I didn't sleep at all that night and even the next morning my dad was telling me that he didn't even want to take me. I was so mad, I needed support for this, and it seemed like nobody cared, or at least they were all against me. I had a peace, from the Lord, I felt safe this time, and I felt that Steven was going to be alright. I had faith like had never had before, I can't even explain the feeling I had, but it was amazing. My dad did end up taking us, since I don't like driving in Los Angeles, and the procedure was the same as before, went into the pre op room, and they wheeled him into the OR. Dr. M was very reassuring, even giving me a hug again and by this time I totally trusted him. I didn't cry this time, I went to the waiting room and waited for a while, then decided to go to the car and get some sleep. I slept for about 4 hours and returned to the waiting room where my dad was. Steven was still in surgery. I was glad that I didn't miss him being in recovery. This surgery took about 6 hours, but I wasn't very nervous, maybe because we had been thru it all before. My biggest concern was if he was going to be able to talk or not. As soon as they called me to tell me that he was in the recovery room, I went straight to him. I waited for a while and he opened his eyes. He had the same head wrap on as in the first surgery, same IV's and the huge one coming out of his neck. I eagerly waited for him to wake up, it seemed like hours but it was really only about 10 minutes. He looked at me and I said "Hi baby, its mommy" he looked a little dazed and he says to me "Kobe, 24". I had to laugh, I was so overjoyed that he could talk, but his first words were the name of his favorite basketball player and his jersey number. I for sure had my same kid back, exactly the way I had sent him into that operating room, but hopefully this time without the drop seizures. Steven was in the PICU for one night and then moved to a regular room, of course we got a shared room again, I always like it when we get the private rooms because there is a couch, and a private bathroom with a bathtub. Steven did very well this time in the hospital, no fevers and he ate really well. He was discharged in 3 days. Recovery at home was similar to the first time, he had a hard time walking, talking and he was vomiting, and again, that was due to the "D" medicine Two days after we were home I realized that he had a swollen red lump on his neck where the big IV had been. This IV from what I understand is a long flexible needle that goes almost to his heart. I guess it's a main vein in your body. Well, I took him to the ER at the hospital in Los Angeles where we were put in the hallway in front of the Trauma Rooms. I always like it when we are put there, although we would prefer a room, but in front of the trauma rooms at least there is something to watch while we are waiting. That night we were there for about 8 hours. It ended up that the site had and infection and there was a small blood clot. The doctors couldn't give him any blood thinners due to the fact that he had just had brain surgery, so we just had to hope that the clot didn't go to his heart. I couldn't believe that he had made it thru brain surgery and something as stupid as a blood clot was putting him at risk. Thankfully it all healed and the clot was never a problem. Steven went about 35 days without a seizure, before he had one, but this time was all different. When Steven would have a seizure before his whole body would shake, a full grand mal. Now, only half of his body was shaking at a time, meaning that the seizures weren't crossing from each hemisphere of the brain. I kept waiting for a drop seizure ,but they never returned, this surgery was a success. The weirdest thing is that after this second surgery, the VNS suddenly started to work. I think it's because Stevens seizures types changed and for some reason it would help to bring him out of a seizure much sooner. Regardless, finally something had been successful.

Stevens first job

I thought I would add this chapter as it was something very special for both Steven and I. Something fun to add to all of the other dramatic stuff that goes on in our lives. Steven continued to do well as far as the seizures are concerned. They did increase over time, but still no drops. Since the seizures had changed, we were able to try different medicines, and even try ones we had previously tried before. Still nothing helped. I was almost at the point where I just wanted to give up. There were no other surgery options, and we tried so many other meds that I was just tired. I tried to do things that would make both of us happy, and would try to forget about the seizures for a while. One day I was online and one of the groups I follow put a post that a pharmaceutical company was looking for a child who had LGS. I sent them my name thinking it was for a clinical trial of a new medicine, which I would jump at the chance to try something new that may help. Well, I received an email I think that same day, and it was actually for a modeling job, and Steven got the part! They needed a new child who actually had LGS and was currently taking their medication for their new ad campaign. I was thrilled, I would have never thought that Steven would have an opportunity like this. I always wanted to be a model growing up, I even was approached several times to come in and do photo shoots, but we never had the money to drive to L.A. and spend the time it took to do it, so as for my dream, well I just got old and so did the dream! Steven was actually approached one time while we were at the horse races! The lady couldn't stop talking about how beautiful he was and gave us her card. I never went in thought because, I knew that Steven couldn't do any acting, let alone sit still for a photo shoot!! Anyways, on the day of the shoot, they sent a limo to drive us out to Los Angeles to a huge photo studio. I always imagined what these places looked like when I was younger and it was nothing like I imagined, it was so much better. The staff from the companies involved were all so nice, they were there at the door to greet Steven when the limo pulled up, and they treated him like a celebrity. They had his favorite music playing on the radio, all of his favorite food, including salad, and to top it off he received some special surprises from his favorite basketball team that the company had purchased for Steven The shoot went great, Steven was like a pro, he even had to have his makeup done. It was an amazing experience and we were so blessed, even just to meet so many caring people who were involved with the whole thing. It's still funny when I see the ad and think "that's my boy". Now he can tell people that he had a job and he was a model, what a great resume that is. I am so proud!

Finally, a break thru

A few chapters back I had mentioned that Steven tried a medicine from Canada with no success. Well, after the years passed and his seizures have changed since the corpus colostomy surgery, we took a chance and tried medicine "O" again. It was actually just by luck that we tried this medicine again, but I will take it, luck or not! Steven went in for a routine VEEG and the doctors found out that he had ESES -electrical status epilepticus during sleep. It basically means that when Steven sleeps, his brain is constantly seizing. I was not too happy to hear this, but hey, it's LGS, what else can I expect? The doctors put Steven on a very high dose of a medicine "V". It seemed to help with the nocturnal seizures until his body became used to it and it didn't work anymore. I was again desperate to get some help for him. We happened to see a new doctor at Stevens next appointment, as Dr. W was in Thailand or something starting an epilepsy clinic. He asked if we had ever tried "O". I told him yes, but would like to give it another try. He agreed and Steven started the next day. He was put on a very high dose to take the place of the medicine "V". I was amazed when this medicine actually worked! My boy was seizure free, well, at least while awake. We had the best summer ever, he didn't have to wear his helmet anymore, I could take him in the store and just let him walk down the aisles and look at things. I felt a freedom for both him and I that I probably had never felt before. I was so grateful for this doctor and this medicine. We made it thru the summer and I started noticing Steven acting up more and more. It got to the point where I was actually afraid of him at times. We were in the car one day and out of nowhere, he grabbed my hair, ripped my dress, bit me, hit me, kicked me, he just was going crazy. He is a lot bigger than me now so I couldn't really defend myself. That was it. I hated to admit it, but I knew it was the "O" that was causing this. I had to make a choice, either the seizures coming back, or the behavior. I had to pick the seizures. It was so hard to "let" the seizures come back. Honestly another one of the hardest decisions I had ever had to make. We managed to get him down to a very low dose of "O" and he seemed to tolerate that dose. The seizures are back, but not as bad. Recently we were able to wean Steven off of one of his other seizure meds, leaving room to add more of the med "O" again. So at this time, we are slowly increasing the dose again. I am praying for another seizure free summer, or even just a little bit of relief with no obnoxious behavior this time!

Behaviors and the teenage years

Lastly, since I had just mentioned Stevens behavior, I most definitely had to write about LGS and the behavior that comes with it. I think the hardest part of LGS is the behavior. Some days I just want to stay in bed and never get up, not having to deal with a child yelling, cussing, kicking, throwing things, but I have to, and I have to face this head on. Steven and others with LGS can get very violent. With LGS a lot of the kids have behavioral issues. They will hit, bite, kick, scream, throw things, you name it. They even shout out curse words, and they really don't know what they are doing. It can be mistaken that it is their faults, or that they are just acting out, when it's actually the LGS. Some of the seizures medications cause behavioral issues and several side effects to go along with the LGS. It can be very frustrating when people are telling you to discipline your child when you know it's not his fault. It's very difficult to understand unless you live it. Some of the kids, well at least with Steven, want constant attention. When I don't have help here at home, I have to be with him at all times. If I leave him to answer a phone call, it's on with him, he will throw something, or go hit my dad, or break something. He always has to be the center of attention. It gets hard when you have to play with a 4 year old in a 15 year old body. I get so tired, I just want to relax or clean my house, but I can't as long as Steven is awake and I am on duty. I just pray that the behavior gets better. There have been times that I just break down and cry, I just can't help it, and it gets so hard. We were at his an appointment to see his cardiologist a few months back and he decided that he didn't want to be there. He starts screaming and calling me a bitch, hitting me, kicking me, in front of everyone. All I could do was just stand there. I turned my back to the people and just started crying. This is the hardest part for me and LGS. We tried several behavioral medications, but they just seem to make him worse. So many people have told me to put him in a group home, but I just can't do that to him. Yes, it is very hard, it's very emotionally draining, but he is my son. I can't live without him, and he needs me. I think people are just worried that he is going to hurt me, which he does at times, but what can I do? He is my son, and I won't turn my back on him ever. These behaviors are just a part of LGS, and I am slowly, and everyday learning how to handle them the best. The behaviors do not make my son, they are just a part of an awful disease, and that is not his fault.

Life Goes On

When I first started writing this book, it was a week before we went to see the fireworks for the Fourth of July, Stevens favorite holiday. I treasure every moment like these, as there were times that I wasn't sure we would ever have these moments. We have our bad days, or very bad days, and we have good days. You just have to take this disease day by day never forgetting that it's your child who has to live with it, and get beaten up by it. Me as the parent, I have to help conquer it, I have to be there for Steven, to care for him, to keep him safe, to love him. So many people have asked me about putting Steven in a care home due to his behavior I know they all mean well, but I don't think that is an option for me, I love him too much, I would miss him too much. He is my only child, he is my life. I understand that is what some parents have to do, and I know it's probably one of the hardest decisions they have had to make, but as of right now, it's not in my plans. I don't know what the future holds for Steven , or for me. All I can do is live in the NOW, and just take everything day by day. I can't guarantee that any medicine is going to work, or that Steven is going to even wake up each morning, all I can do is have FAITH and trust in God that he has his hand on Steven. I hate this disease, I wish there was more awareness for LGS, let alone epilepsy. People need to know that this is real, not just something people make fun of or that you see in movies. Our kids are real people suffering with this disorder, real parents heartbroken when our children are seizing uncontrollably and we can't help them. I just hope that by writing this, I can bring some kind of awareness, thru my story, others can see that this is real, and it doesn't get enough attention, as it should. Even if I can help a parent who is new to this and looking for some help, I want them to know that you are not alone. I just want to thank you for reading this, I had been wanting to do this for some time, but I didn't think anyone would really want to read it. After much thought and some Opinions of friends, I decided to just write and see what happens. I just hope it will touch you and help others to understand what a beast this LGS really is.

The following are some journal entries that I make on a regular basis regarding Steven. I thought I would include what I them so that you can get more of a personal feel of daily life living with LGS.

June 18, 2010

Well, this is my first journal entry, I wish I had started this a long time ago!! Anyways, Steven had his 2nd brain surgery on May 28th. It has been 3 weeks, and so far so good. No Grand mals!! Hopefully they got lost and don't come back!! We had a really rough 3 weeks w/recovery though. He had been vomiting and not holding anything down. Had to go to the ER at the hospital the day after he was released cause he had a central line infection, luckily, after about 4 days it was gone..ohh, but all the oozy yellow stuff coming out..yuck!! Anyways, the vomiting..we went to the ER by my house and they did a ct scan that looked like there was a little fluid in the brain, but they didn't have anything to compare it to see if it was new or not. I took him to the hospital this week so the neurosurgeon could compare the CT and he said it looked fine. His neurologist said that the med "D" they put him on after surgery was most likely the cause for the vomiting because it makes his other meds out of whack, and he had signs of overdose. So...we took him off and he is doing wonderful so far. He finally ate today, and yesterday..and is holding it down. He is still pretty weak, not walking on his own without me holding him, but he is coming around. Just like the first time, I know it will take about 6 months for him to get back to baseline. So here we are again on this journey that I thought I would never be on again...but hey, if there is even a little slight chance it could help him, I had to do it and I am glad I did , regardless of the outcome.

July 6, 2010
well, it is now 35 days post op for Steven and he is continuing to do well. We had a small episode the other night, I think it was a partial seizure, but it was so small..his little hand just went out and then he was trying to put it into his mouth. He is smiling more than I have ever seen him smile, and laughing...it's nice to have that back. He is enjoying summer time in CA in his swimming pool, and is turning into a tan kid!! He tells me "mom, I'm tan"..anyways, just wanted to write a little update while I was here visiting another site

July 14. 2010
Well my little guy turned 13 on July 12th. I can't believe he is a teenager!! I am so proud of him, he has came such a long way. As far as post op it had been 44 days, and no grand mals. He has

had a partial, I don't know what kind of partial since I am not very familiar with partials yet. His head turned toward the right and then it just stopped, which I was so glad because the seizures are not crossing over. So far, it's only movement on his right side. He has an appt on the 20th to meet with the neurologist so I am hoping to find out what kind of seizures these are. I am so glad I made the decision to do the second surgery. Steven is doing so much better. He will actually sit and not run around constantly. He seems a lot calmer, I can't wait for him to go back to school and see how he progresses. I just keep faith and keep saying that he is healed, I am not letting these small seizures get me down. I do see some of his old behaviors coming back slowly though, like staring at the wall, smacking his feet together, making squeaking noises on stuff, but it is not as bad as before. He does repeat words over and over and over....which sometimes can be so annoying. but I am just glad he is talking!! Hopefully it is just his brain adjusting to not being able to communicate. So, all in all..he is doing great. Going to take him to Del mar next week and see how he does at the beach. I can't wait because we haven't been able to go to the beach in quite some time because the heat really triggered grand mals, so we will see how that goes!!! OK, well I will try to keep all of you up to date, there is not much really going on right now..but that it a good thing since we are only a little over 1 month post op. I will let you know how the neuro appt goes!!! Oh, the picture I added is from his birthday party...he had a Lakers party and was soooo excited to get a real basketball!!

July 21, 2010
Well, Steven had his first follow up with the neurologist

yesterday. He had had a partial seizure on Saturday, it was only the right side, but it was a pretty big one. Anyways, the his doctor asked me if I wanted to keep his meds the same since he was not doing that bad, and I asked her if any of the AED's he was currently on were for partials. She said they were mostly to treat Grand Mals, so I asked if there was something we could try that helped partials. She put him on med "K". Steven has been on "K" in the past, about 6 years ago and it made him soooo hyper that I had to stop it. I figured that this time he is older and maybe it wouldn't be the same this time, so he is back on it. His first dose was last night, and this morning he was a little off balance, and had just a little more energy, but nothing bad..yet!!! We increase it over the next 3 weeks so we will just have to wait and see how it goes!!! He was really excited because he got a magazine that had a story about his neurosurgeon in it, he has been showing it to everyone!!! So, now its bedtime and I am laying here with him waiting for him to fall asleep so I can finally relax myself!!! Will keep updating as I'm sure there will be much more to come!!

September 2, 2010

Well, Steven is doing alright. He is on "K" since his last doctors visit, and it seems to help a little. I don't know if it is the surgery or the med, but his seizures are way less severe and not as frequent. He started the 8th grade last week ,and he is loving being back in school, I have to take him late each day because his meds make him too tired to participate in anything in the morning. So, that's about it for now, not much to report, just taking it day by day and crossing my fingers that I never see a grand mal again!!!

November 3, 2010

It has been a while! Steven has been better. Since his surgery in May, we took him to the hospital for a 24 hr VEEG. It showed that he is having seizures on both sides of his brain, but..they aren't crossing over, which means the surgery was successful. He is having partial seizures which is good because now there are more meds that we can try that we couldn't use before. The neuro put him on med "T", and we took him off of the "K". He is having about 1 seizure a day ,but some days he may have 6 or more. He is doing pretty well except this sudden increase in behavior I don't know if it's just him being a teenager, or all the meds, but something has to be done soon!! So, luckily right now, things are mostly calm. I am trying to raise money to take him back to Key Largo to swim w/the dolphins (where he went on his make a wish trip)...hopefully I will get enough to take him in June!! I am thinking of taking him to Disneyland in Dec..it will be 6 months post op (which is how long the doc said I have to wait to take him)...so he hopefully will like that!! Stevens aid at school wrote to the Lakers to see if we could get Steven to go to a game..hopefully that works out as well!!! So, just trying to stay busy and keep the kiddo happy while we are having some down time!! Will keep you posted as things progress!!

Mar 18, 2011

I didn't realize how long it has been since I have updated, but you all know how it is!! Steven is doing better in regards to his seizures, they are now partial complex, but much better than the full on Gran Mals. We have been going thru these rage episodes, which I found out may be rage seizures. It is hard to handle, especially since he is soooo strong, but by the grace of God, I am getting thru it. We are going to be taking Steven to a behavioral neurologist to see if she can be of some help with the behavior Other than that, he is doing pretty well, we get his post op MRI done early April, and hopefully everything healed nicely!! OK ,keeping it short because my sweetie is ready for bed now, all of the meds kicking in!!! Talk to ya soon! :)

May 2, 2011

I swear, it takes me forever to remember to updated Stevens journal!! Well, Steven has been very moody lately. I don't know if it's just him being a teenager or the fact that his VNS battery is getting low. Ya, I signed the consent for surgery to have it replaced, he is getting the new model, which is much smaller..just waiting for a surgery date. His seizures continue every day, still no luck with them, but we do see the neurologist this week so maybe we can figure something out w/meds. I also have been really thinking about putting Steven back on the keto diet for the 3rd time..we never got to go thru with it for the whole 2 years. We will see how it goes!! Anyways, just a short update for now!!!

July 5, 2011

wow..it has been a while since I have updated, as usual. I am so used to posting little tid bits of our daily happenings on facebook that I forget to come on here and write it all down. Well, Steven is..well..the same I guess. He had his new VNS implanted last month, only to have to go back in 3 days later and have it re-opened because the lead wire was loose and they had to tighten it back. I am not so sure that the new VNS is working as well as the old one. It seems like the seizures are more often since the surgery. He was doing soooo well before, he went I think it was 4 days without a seizure. Who knows, it also could be because we added med "L", I just hate the seizures. This week, he threw up 4 times at night only, he would wake up and vomit and go back to sleep, I am thinking abdominal seizures. I really can't believe how many types of seizures there are, it never ends. So anyways, not much new to report, just riding this roller coaster called LGS. Taking Steven to the circus for the first time this month w/starlight foundation, it think it will be fun for him, and especially because it is at the staples center where his favorite Lakers play!!! I just love to see him smile and would do anything to see his smile!! Oh, his birthday is in 7 days, he is going to be 14, I can't believe I have a 14 year old..thank God that Steven isn't out doing what I was doing when I was his age..lol...I love my little sweet boy!!!

August 16, 2011

ok, it has been a while..as with all my CB posts!! lol!! It's been a long month for us. Steven has been doing as good as can be expected, but I am always so thankful that is just happy and he doesn't let the seizures effect him, heck..I don't know if he even knows he has seizures. As for me, I feel like I am loosing it. Seriously!! I would have bet everything that his VNS was messed up, but after Dr. M (the neurosurgeon) looked at the x-rays (which weren't very good btw..) and actually checking the VNS..he said it's just fine. He said it's at 2 and 2.5 whatever that means and goes off every 14 seconds..so it does need to be increased. But I HATE it when I am wrong when it comes to Steven because I am usually right!! lol!! So now it's in the neurologists hands. Stevens seizures are not more frequent, just stronger. And the other day he started a right sided seizure..It stopped, about 2 seconds later a left sided seizure started..this has happened twice now. I am suspecting that it could be the fact that we are taking him off of med "F" because of his rage episodes. The fact is though, I am not going to stop taking him off of the "F" because I am starting to see a glimpse of my sweet boy. Not a very big glimpse..just a little sparkle!!*, but I just want that back, that boy that is loving and not mad all of the time. So then I realized that his med "L" was supposed to have been up to 100 mg and I only went to 50 mg 2xday...I couldn't figure out why the RX was lasting so long..haha..I don't know where my head has been, but so now..I am increasing the other 50mg's morn and night over the next 3 weeks..I am praying this gives some relief to the seizures. what else...oh..I had put on facebook how I was concerned about Stevens testicles (it's so weird to write about my sons parts.lol)..but one was like the size of a walnut and the other the size of a grape..so we went and had an ultrasound and we go to get the results tomorrow..I am praying that everything is alright. Oh, and yesterday when we went to see the neurosurgeon, it was kind of sad. Sad because we basically told his surgeon goodbye :(..he had said that since there are no more surgeries that are an option for Steven he would see us when the vns battery needs replaced (which is usually 6-8 yrs)...well Steven is 14 and by the time it needs replaces he will be at least 18 and no longer able to be a pediatric patient..:(..it's so funny how the doctors can become like family. I told him that he will be in the new "B" med add and we will come by and have Steven autograph it...he laughed and said to do it!! At least he won't forget Steven!! lol!! So, Steven starts school on the 23rd..I am excited for him to go back, I know he has been so bored this summer. His 1:1 aide came by today to visit and bring him a birthday gift..it was nice to see her, Steven ran so fast to the door..it was funny. Wow.i think this is the longest update I have ever written...I guess I just have a lot to say this time!! haha!! Well, nothing else I can think of, but I will keep you all posted (if anyone actually reads my posts..lol) on how the ultrasound goes!!!

September 8, 2011

It's been a long month this month!! Steven started 9th grade, which is supposed to be his first year of high school, but the school here is very good about keeping the more severe kids in the middle school for as long as possible. He really loves school, and he is not in his wheelchair this year!!! I sent it last year because he had an accident and had to get stitches, and I wanted to protect him, but he can walk...and this year I am determined to have him do so. We also moved last week, got a smaller house, but it is a 3 bdrm so now we all have our own rooms!! Stevens room is decorated all in Lakers and he has his signed Kobe jersey on the wall (he got it from the photo shoot he did w/"B" as well as a signed Lakers basketball!)...I got him a new purple comforter for his bed, he has the bean bag, and his dresser is painted purple and gold!! Go Lakers!! lol...In the mean time, I have been just so stressed..My uncle is still in jail, it's a long story...and Stevens and I'm not getting answers regarding Steven!! I am so frustrated w/the hospital right now. I am so used to getting preferential treatment..lol..and now they are just treating Steven like any other patient!!! :(haha..I know, it's selfish, but I can't ever get thru on the phone to make an appt, and so I have always emailed them to get one, and I usually get in within a week or 2. This time they said I can't bring him in until Oct. 31st!! I just want to start the diet, and have the VNS increased...how hard is that?? I know how to do all of the diets, and even the keto w/Steven I don't have to start in the hosp, they let me do it at home because I have done it before and Steven can't fast when he starts it. I think I am to the point where I want to give another hospital in Orange County a try again. Steven is much older now, he was 4 when we last went there. It's not like they have to diagnose him, or do any surgeries..Etc..It's all been done. I don't think they are going to have the miracle cure for him, which I don't think that's ever going to come...so why waste my time driving 2 hrs and over 200 miles round trip going to Los Angeles when I can just drive to O.C and go to that hospital? Steven has an appt on Oct. 12 w/metabolics at in O.C..I wanted to take him back to where his records are from when he was little. I want to find out what was wrong w/him as a newborn. I know that he had hypoglycemia for 3 weeks and was in the NICU for 3weeks, but I don't know why I kept going there for 2 yrs after he was born. They had mentioned mitochondrial disorder, but at the time they were basically just watching him I think..but the seizures started and LGS took over...it was all about fixing Steven, and fixing the seizures...lol..when I look back, I had no clue what I was in for!!! Anyways, if they do find something w/metabolics I may just go ahead and change the neuro as well so his treatment is all at the same hospital. It's only for 4 more years, then he will be 18 and we have to see adult docs then. Oh, and Steven is doing much better since we have been taking off some of his meds (w/the neuros permission of course, but I TOLD her I was going to do it and she said I could!)...amazing how much better he is without some of them!!! he is now on 4 seizure meds (well 5, but "F" is gone in 2 1/2 weeks). OK, well I am rambling on...just wanted to update, or I guess more like vent!!!!

September 19, 2011

<u>My prayer</u>....Dear God,

I know that I haven't been the best in my life, I have done so many things that I know you had to forgive me for. But when it comes to Steven, I pray Dear God that you help him. Give me strength to deal with this awful disease. God, you know, there are days that I wonder how I can keep going on, and I cry to you and beg you to make things better. I have asked you why it had to be my son, why me? I know that you have a plan for both of us. I know that you love Steven, and that he is one of yours. God, I feel like I am losing my mind right now. So much going on in my life at this time, and I hold to you to make it better. I know that there are struggles, it's just how it is. When it comes to my son, though, God...I hate to think of anything happening to him. I hate to have to make tough decisions for him, I hate for him to hurt, yet at the same time I see him smile, and make his funny remarks and think to myself "why would I want to "fix" him..he is perfect the way he is. He is happy, and he knows you God, he tells everyone about you and Jesus..he knows. God I <u>just pray</u> that you lead me in the right direction when it comes to anything to do with Steven I know that I can't do it myself, I need you. I know your will be done no matter what, and I trust in You. God give me patience, Faith and Hope. I just ask that you help me to cry when I need to, I haven't cried in so long, help me to let it out. Just always be with us God, in Jesus Name I ask...Amen.

December 10, 2011

Well, this will be a short entry but is much easier for me to just write it all here then post several comments on facebook. So on Dec. 8th, we went in for an overnight VEEG...neuro team came in the next day and said that we needed to stay another night to see whets going on while he is sleeping. Stevens actual neurologist came in (she NEVER comes in when we are in the hospital)..she said that there were spikes on the EEG that they didn't know what they were, they weren't seizures...although there was seizure activity on there as well. She explained that she was going to give Steven a VERY high dose of "V" to see if it helps, she said that it could help with his cognitive skills as well. So, ok...I said yes, and he got the dose last night. No seizures at least that were visible last night or all day today. neuro team came back in to release him and said that I should call Dr. W on Monday, that they were going to have a Steven meeting and even bring in the neurosurgeon to look at the MRI from his surgery...I knew something was going on, but I wasn't quite sure. He said that they wanted Steven to come back in a month for another VEEG to see if the "V" has helped. So we packed up and left. On the way home, I looked at his discharge papers and it said "diagnosis:

LGS and ESES" WHAT???? they added a diagnosis and I had no idea...I guess what ESES is , is non convulsive static epilepticus during sleep...so of course I had to look it up on the internet, I really don't understand anything except it is very rare, like 0.5% of kids w/epilepsy have this, I don't know if it can be fixed, and I don't even know if he for sure has this...but I just done know what to think at this point. I am not angry, scared or anything, I think I am numb to stuff like this, I just like to be informed. So anyways, Steven got his evening dose of his "V" tonight..he is on 20 mg now (it was 40 mg last night)..he is sleeping and I am hoping for another seizure free night and day tomorrow. Will try to update more often on here.

December 16, 2011

I think I posted last time that we were going in for a VEEG. Well they hooked Steven all up (they actually had a bed ready and waiting for the first time ever). He had the overnight VEEG and so the next morning, Steven as usual pulled all of the leads off, and I figured, well we are going home anyways..so no big deal. Wait..let me back up a bit...the first day, a new neurologist that I had never met before came in and was the head of the neuro team this time Dr. C. He was very interested in Steven, which I am not used to that. Steven is pretty much old news, one of those kids who they can't do anything for anymore, just one of those kids with LGS. Anyways, he was very interested in him, asking him about his problems as a newborn and basically his whole history, I don't know, there was just something different about this guy. He was very interested in the fact that I had taken Steven to the hospital in O.C to get metabolic testing done and that the doctor had ordered a DNA test to check for NKTH (non ketotic hyperglycinemai), he wanted to talk to the dr at the other hospital. I even told my dad that I was surprised at how interested he was in Steven, I am not used to this. So, now I can continue from before..we were ready to go home, just waiting for the neuro team to come in and they came in and said that Steven had and abnormal VEEG and that he had to stay overnight again. The doctor said that they didn't know what was going on, they had never seen anything like it..I was scared, I didn't know what was going on..anyways the doctor leaves, and later that night he gets 40mg "V" dose. I didn't see any visible seizures, I don't know how to read the VEEG so if he was still seizing, and I had no clue. The next day, no seizures. The neuro Dr. C came in w/the team and as he was explaining the release orders he kept looking at the VEEG, he said "its still the same", I have no idea what that meant..but he looked at it several times like he was confused. He said to call Dr. W in 2 days to see the results of the 2nd night VEEG (he said they hadn't had a chance to go over it yet) and to give Steven 20mg Valium per night. We left and while I was in the car, I saw on the discharge papers under diagnosis "LGS, and ESES"...huh?? what the heck was ESES? nobody told me about this. So of course I quickly googled it from my phone and it said it is basically non convulsive status epilepticus during sleep. I didn't read anything about this really being associated with LGS, but rather a different disorder called NKH (can't think of what it stands for at the moment)..made me wonder if maybe Steven is misdiagnosed and thatch why for 14 years they haven't ever been able to help him. I don't know, I think I just get all kinds of thoughts thru my head when it comes to Steven. So I waited 3 days and never heard from the neuro and so I finally emailed her. I asked her about the ESES and told her that Steven hadn't seized since the "V" dose. I heard nothing back. So I waited 3 more days, emailed her again and told her that Steven was 6 days seizure free...I got a response "good to know". So I don't know whets going on rite now, I wish I could find out somehow, but am just going to be patient. Steven did finally have a seizure on that 6th day, he took a nap and had a seizure while sleeping, it wasn't

very strong or long, but I was bummed that he had one. I think it was because it was at about 3 and his "V" dose was long gone at that time of day. He had another tonight, but it was right as he fell asleep, I had just given him his Valium dose and it probably hadn't hit him yet..so at least I think I know what is going on w/that. I took him this week and finally got that DNA test done, we will get the results in 6 to 8 weeks, our appt in O.C is on Feb 22nd so I am hoping to get some answers w/that as well.
..So...lol.. that was my last couple of weeks..lol..luckily Steven doesn't have a clue and I am glad that he don't have to stress about it all like his mama does. I guess I don't even have to stress, but I am his only advocate, I am the one who has to stand up for him, protect him..it is my job so if stress comes along w/it..then hey, that's just the way it goes. Alright, I think this is the longest post I have ever posted..haha..I guess I had a lot to say this time, but I will close for now and hopefully next update will be some better news and not as long :)

December 25, 2011

Well, I don't know if anyone actually reads my posts..but I like to write them anyways. Today is Christmas...Steven had a very nice Christmas over 3 days. I had him open his gifts on Friday since we weren't going to be home over the weekend. Saturday we spent w/my brother and today was at my grandmas..it was long weekend. The bad part...Steven had had some of the worst seizures he has had in a long time, so much for the "V" being our miracle. He woke up today having 3 grand mals (partials, I think)..right in a row. Last night he had 2 back to back..they were bad..his face twitching..the gasping for air..I felt so bad for him and I feel so helpless. It always seems like when something is finally helping the LGS comes in to steal it away. He also has a little head cold so he want feeling to good today, he just kind of sat around, not like his usual hyper self. I felt so bad for him, I saw our little cousins out running and playing in the backyard, having fun..and poor Steven is always stuck inside with the adults. The kids don't really talk to him, its not their faults, they really don't understand Steven or how to approach him, they are much younger than him. But, it makes me wonder if he feels, or does he even realize that he isn't out there playing as he should be? I hope not. I just hope that someday he can be out there playing too..running and laughing, and getting dirty..just being a boy. I hate seizures, I hate how they take away from my sons life, I hate that nobody can fix him. What I do know though, is...that God has a plan for Steven, I may not know it..in fact...I don't know it...but God does and it wont be like this forever. I know that Steven is happy and very well taken care of and that's most important. I am praying that in this new year coming that he finally gets his miracle and these seizures will stop, I hope that instead of him sitting on a couch by his aunt, or uncle or mom...that he too, will be out with the kids playing. My prayer for the new year is just for him..for Gods grace to be upon him, his mercy and his healing. So...with that...I think its time for mommy to get some sleep..gonna cuddle my sweet guy and have another beautiful day with him tomorrow, and be thankful that I have him, and that he is the boy that he is♥♥

February 22, 2012

Well, I think I put it in my last journal post, but I don't think anyone reads these, but if you do..thanks. This is just my way of getting out stuff that is getting to me, or just going on in our lives. I posted on facebook about today but there is only so much you can put in a facebook status update. Honestly, really honestly...I am just in give up mode. Let me go back a bit, back in October I took Steven to O.C to have some metabolic testing done. In my heart I KNEW that this was the answer, I knew that the test would show something and Stevens seizures would stop. I have been waiting for 4 months for these test results to change our lives forever. Today, that didn't happen. I don't want to sound ungrateful, because other than Stevens seizures, I have a perfectly healthy little boy..but I was almost ready to cry when the metabolic specialist came in and told me that all tests were negative. They tested for so many disorders I cant even tell you, they tested his DNA, fatty chain amino acids, even for the syndrome that the guy in lorenzos oil had (I don't remember what it was)...and NOTHING. Like I said, that is a good thing, but it brings me no closer to my dreams of making Steven better. I felt so hopeless today, I wanted to go to his neurologist and just scream "FIX MY SON"...I wanted to sue the the hospital that caused him to have seizures in the first place..(the let him stay inside me while his heart rate was dropping for 12 hours before someone decided to do a cesarean.ya..his umbilical cord was around his neck 5 times, he was suffocating..lack of oxygenate which can lead to seizures, and all the low blood sugar issues he had as a newborn)..anyways, I wanted to lash out at someone today, but nobody to lash out to. I held in my tears because I have cried so many times that I can't cry anymore, I just had that feeling in me that I wanted to kick something, or hit something...but what can I do but hold it together for Steven I have to remember that he don't know any of this, he don't think that he is any different than anyone else. So after leaving the doctors I went to my grandmas..I feel so bad because we go there and Steven usually just sits in a chair and basically gets ignored. I mean, we all try to talk to him, but he has to stay in the living room cause of the darned seizures, he can't be left alone to go play, or do anything. But he sits there patiently, while we all catch up and talk about stuff that really doesn't even matter. Then it's a long 2 hour drive home where again, he is by himself in the back seat playing with his tag book in the dark, sitting with his legs bent up on the seat cause my car is too small for my growing boy. It breaks my heart. I want so much more for him, I want him to be able to go the park and run as fast as he can and play until he can't play anymore. But he can't, because any excitement, or anything that gets his heart rate going brings on a seizure. Last week my aunts friend was playing with Steven pretending that Steven was scaring him..Steven was laughing so hard, it was nice to see him laugh, but it all ended when a seizure stopped it..he can't even have a good time because it the seizures It's NOT fair to him..I hate seizures, I hate LGS, I am mad at the doctors for not doing more, and I ask God "Why"..not why does Steven have seizures, but why wont he heal Steven? what else do I need to do? I know that I have to WAIT..because God isn't telling me no, but to just wait, but I have been waiting for 14 years, I am tired of waiting. I honestly don't know what to do next. I mentioned IVIG to his neuro, I didn't get a very convincing answer, I mentioned IVIG to his metabolic dr. he said it's very controversial and that it may not even work. Do they not understand that I would let them inject monkey enzymes in Steven if there was a CHANCE that it could help him..I don't care if the treatment isn't proven..let me try it. We go to see his neurologist in April, and I just am burnt out..I'm tired of the same old increase/decrease meds routine, I don't even feel like trying the keto diet for the 3rd time. I honestly feel like I am done searching..I am just going to live life as it is. I don't think I can keep getting my hopes up just to be let down..it never fails, it's always a let down. The only thing that has ever helped Steven is friggen proactiv...lol..and that isn't even for seizures..lol..but do you know how good it feels for SOMETHING to actually work?? I will take what I can get. So, enough of me venting, I just needed to get it all out, I couldn't wait to get home and write this, it helps so much, even if I am just writing to myself. Steven is sleeping, and I think I am going to get some rest as well. It has been such a long day and I need to wake up to a brighter day tomorrow, and not get my hopes up anymore.

March 6, 2012

Well, I don't have much of anything new going on except the same old seizure stories. On Saturday Steven had the worst seizure he has ever had. We had been out shopping that day, it wasn't that hot, maybe about 79..a nice day. We got home and ate lunch and I let him go outside and play with his buckets (he likes to put dirt in the buckets w/a shovel) There is no shade in my backyard, and the sunlight was pretty hot as he was directly in it. He had a small seizure so I told him we had to go inside. We were in about 10 minutes, and he was sitting in the chair at the kitchen table, and bam..seizure. I thought it was just his regular seizure, I pulled him out of the chair and laid him on the floor. I didn't have his VNS magnet w/me..but I figured by the time I got it he would be out of the seizure. It kept going..I had my dad come into the room and after about 5 mins I got the med "D",which is a rectal rescue med. HE HAS NEVER had a shaking episode for more than a minute. His head raised up and his whole face turned blue during this one, which has never happened either. The "D" stopped that part of the seizure, but afterward was the worst. Its funny cause to most people the shaking part would be most scary, but us moms who go thru this, it is after that you have to worry about the most. Steven laid there, gurgling and breathing very deep. His heart was racing, and I got a cold rag and put it on his head. His pupils were fixed and dilated, there was no response from him. I moved him to the couch hoping that he would come out of it, but he didn't by this time it was about 10 mines into it. He just laid there on the couch, no response, then he took a deep breath and then stopped breathing (or so it seemed). My heart dropped, I thought "this is it". He seemed like he just wasn't there brain wise, I did ask him to squeeze my hand and he slightly did w/his right hand, but he couldn't with his left hand. My dad told me to call the ambulance, but since we are only about 5 mins from the hospital I thought it would be easier to just get him in the car and drive ourselves. We each got a side of him and got him in the car. I noticed that while in the car he still couldn't use his left arm. Anyways, by the time we got him in the hospital he started to come out of it. There is nothing that they can do for as seizure, so I waited until I knew he was back to normal and we left. The next day he did very good, no big seizures. He had about 10 seizures this morning, but nothing the rest of the day. Now, tonight..he is seizing in his sleep. he will open his eyes, and you can see them twitching. Then he closes them. His head will sometimes turn to the side, and he actually had 2 seizures that I could see while he was sleeping. I AM SO SICK of this. I want these things to stop. Poor Steven can't even go outside and play. My house is like a tomb, I have black out curtains over all of my blinds so the sunlight doesn't get in. He is so looking forward to me putting up the pool this summer, but I am not so sure about that now. I feel so bad because I hold back so much from him because I want him to be safe and I want to reduce the risk of seizures. This just sucks. We need a cure. Inst it crazy that epilepsy has been around since the bible was written?? and they still are no closer to a cure than they were back then. Sometimes I think they don't even try to find a cure, since kids like ours keep the drug companies in business. Anyways, I better hear from his neuro soon, or I am..well, I don't know what I am going to do..lol..I really want to tell her to admit him and take all these meds off and start from scratch. I was reading emails from 2008 (I save every single email, just cause there are lots of med changes etc. and I want to always have proof that the dr. allowed me to decrease or add meds)..but there were meds I had forgotten he was on, "Z", and "T", (well I knew he was on it when he was 4, but forgot we tried it a second time)..it was crazy reading over the emails, all the med changes, the diets, the surgeries..almost sickening. I think I should write a book, seriously. Well, that's it for now, Steven is breathing weird so I have to change his position. Love to you all, and God bless.

March 11, 2012

Yes, as I said in my title, this is such a long road. We spent 2 nights in the hospital this week at the hospital. Stevens seizures just wouldn't stop. Not so much the grand mals, but the absence were terrible. He just wasn't there. The doctors there said they wanted to try a new medicine on him, well, it's an old med, but new for Steven It's called "P". I guess it's like another med he has been on before. They said they wanted to monitor him. I told the doctors that he probably wouldn't have many seizures in the hospital because he is not around his "triggers". And of course, he didn't have many, so the docs think this med is helping. Today, of course it was back to seizures like normal, he had a bad one on the toilet, of course I was there to help him so he didn't hurt himself. I am so tired of this, I feel like I am 80 yrs old, I think my grandma at 81 probably has more energy than I do. I wasn't feeling very confident in this new med in the first place, and now it's just another toxin in his body. I may try him on this juice stuff, I ordered 4 bottles of it, actually me and my dad are going to try it first, then start giving it to Steven slowly. It's some kind of seaweed based drink, supposed to help w/all kinds of illnesses, and my uncle actually went to a convention for the company and talked to a man that had seizures and took this juice and he no longer has seizures. I don't know how frequent he had seizures, I'm going to call the guy when I get a chance tomorrow and find out more, but I'm down to the natural stuff, because none of these meds are ever going to help him. I even signed up to be a "seller" of this juice, and if it works for Steven, even a little you better believe I will share it with all of you. Anyways, I am waiting for Steven to go to sleep, I need to take a shower sooo bad..lol..just wanted to update while I am sitting here waiting for him. Hopefully soon I will have better news to post.

March 23, 2012

Well, I had some free time tonight so thought I would write. Since Steven was in the hospital 2 weeks ago, nothing much has changed. At first I thought the new med, "P" was helping w/his seizures, but it's not..his seizures are the same as usual. His behavior is worse though. Not so much at home, has been acting up at school. Breaking things, saying mean things to other kids...just being plain mean. I am having a meeting at his school in a few weeks to discuss this issue. I really am at a loss when it comes to this because I think most of it is from the meds he is on. I can't just take him off of them (well, the neuro gave me permission today to take one of the doses off)..but I don't think that there are any answers to Stevens behavior There are so many issues that contribute to it. He is a teenager, which I know is a big contributor, but he went thru puberty at about 12 and he is almost 15. There is the meds, I bet if anyone took just 1 of Stevens pills they would be pretty agitated too. Then there is LGS...I don't know how anyone thinks they can fix this situation. I have learned to live with it, I accept Steven even with his little tantrums he has, and it's not an easy thing, and I can understand at school it is probably hard for them. All I can do is print as much info on LGS, and his med side effects as possible and bring it all w/me. It's a little frustrating, but what can I do? He is going to be going to the high school next year and I hope they are as tolerant as the middle school has been. At least I know one of the aides at the high school, and I am sure she will be a little partial to Steven :) (she used to be his 1:1 aid in elementary school). Anyways, hoping things start looking up for him, he already has to deal with seizures every day, and anyone should be able to be sympathetic to what he goes thru, but to add the behavioral issues with it is just another to add to his plate. He is a sweet boy, and I know he don't mean the things he says. I feel bad as a parent, because I don't teach him this stuff, and it makes me look as if I teach him these words when I don't. I don't even cuss, ok, well maybe I might say the "s" word from time to time..lol..but I don't teach Steven to be like this, and I know he can't help it. OK ,well enough for now, I am going to finish crocheting my purple scarf to wear for epilepsy awareness day.

April 4, 2012

Today my sweet boy is sick :(...I know it sounds so stupid to say he has a head cold, but this kid NEVER gets sick, hardly even a runny nose. He is coughing due to the drainage from his sinuses. I feel so bad for him, because when he coughs, he thinks he has to throw up, I think from the CC surgery, his brain thinks he has to throw up. Anyways, he has been out of school all week, but of course he doesn't mind that. I think the issues w/behavior and school are finally figured out after a call from the LGS foundation to the teacher, I think he understands that Stevens behaviors can't be avoided and that they are not his fault. Tomorrow I take Steven to Los Angeles to see a fellow doctor on the team (his reg. neuro is in China starting a clinic). I am hoping that he will step up and do something since he has been clustering every night and more grand mals, I am crossing my fingers that he isn't afraid to "mess" with Steven since he isn't his regular neurologist. Well, just a short little update for now, not much to update, I guess that's a good thing. Will let everyone know how the doctors appt. goes tomorrow.

April 5, 2012

Wow, 2 entries in a row..I'm on a roll..lol. Well, I was going to put this update on facebook ,but it's so much easier on here. So, we went to Los Angeles today, found out that my uncle is still in the hospital there, so we were able to visit him. He had a liver transplant about a year ago, and is in there for some other reasons, of course I wasn't able to visit because Steven is sick, but my dad got to have a nice visit with him. Anyways, today we saw Dr. S, he is a younger doctor, and very nice as usual w/the neuro team at that hospital. He told me that the reason the "V" isn't working on Steven anymore is because it metabolizes very fast and with Stevens tolerance that's why the seizures are back at night, so there would really be no reason to increase it, because we would just have to keep increasing. He suggested med "O", he said it's in the same family (benzo) as "V" but works differently, so I agreed. Steven was on "O" about 6 yrs ago, I honestly don't remember whether it was him being hyper on it, or that it didn't work, or if it was the fact that we had to get it from Canada and pay cash each month for it, for the reason we stopped it. He was only on it about a week or two, but I figured since its available now in the USA, I would give it a try again. So the "O" (clobazam) will replace the "V" at night, and if tolerated we will add another dose in the morning as well, starting at 20 mg each dose. Also, because "P" and "P" are basically the same thing (M turns into P after it goes thru your system), we are taking off the M and increasing the P from 30 mg to 45mg 2xday. Hopefully if all of this helps and is tolerated, we will start taking off the "K" (YAY). The doctor said Steven is on to many benzos and they need to be decreased, hey, I'm up for any decrease, or change..lol..I get sick of the same ol same ol, all the time. He also increased his VNS to go off every 1.8 minutes, so basically it goes off 8 times in 10 minutes. So glad to have some adjustments today, and hopefully we can get all of this done soon. I have to wait for his "P" levels before we can start the increase, and I have to wait for the "O" to be approved and ordered at our pharmacy, so it's looking like sometime next week we will start the changes. Dr. M (another neuro on the team) came in as well, and she had to say hello to her famous patient..lol..she saw Stevens "B" ad in the ped neuro journal...lol. I am going to have to get him to autograph some pics to give to all the docs. I almost want to keep seeing this doctor, but we have been with Dr. W for

10 years not and I trust her completely with Steven, so we will continue to see her, it was just nice to have another opinion for a change. Steven sees Dr. W on the 30th, so hopefully we will be far in this med change at that time. After a nice 4 hour drive home thanks to L.A. traffic, Steven is in bed, all rubbed down with Vicks and hopefully will get some sleep tonight, this cold has been awful for him, he never ever ever gets sick, this must have been a strong one going around. So until next time, as always, keep my kiddo in your prayers and hopefully next post will be some great news that the "O" is working.

May 6, 2012

Well, it will be one month on May 9th that Steven started "O". He has been seizure free while he is AWAKE for almost a whole month. The status seizures continue while he is SLEEPING, but since we increased "O" about a week ago, they are not as bad. It's so hard to get my hopes up, but I will tell you what, I am LOVING this so far. It's nice to take him in a store WITHOUT his helmet (of course I am holding his hand or he is not far from me). He loves going to stores and looking at all the toys, taking his time and me backing off and letting him have some independence while it lasts. I really hope it does, I have had so many let downs with other meds that work for a while then stop, that's why I am taking every moment in with this. The ONLY downside, is that he is a little more agitated, I guess, if that's what you would call it. His attention span is not very long, which it always has been short, but it's a little shorter now. Maybe because he is not seizing he wants to do everything, I don't know. He is sleeping much better, he actually sleeps in until about 8 or 9, compared to waking up at 2, 4 , 5, 6..etc. So that is

VERY nice. He goes to sleep a little later, instead of 6, it's about 7 or 8, I can't complain. He actually talked on the phone with my sister the other day, it was so neat, cause she used to talk to him all the time when he was little, and all these years, he will only listen or say a couple of words..so it was a new milestone for him. It has been a little harder on me, of course, he is wanting to do what HE wants to do instead of me telling him everything to do, and at the same time, that teenager attitude is coming out and its worse than the terrible twos..lol. Oh..and, he gained almost 10 lbs since he started "O"...which is good because this kid had a hard time gaining weight, I couldn't believe that I had to go to the men's section to buy him shorts the other day. I am a little worried, because he REALLY can eat. Today he ate, within 2 hours, 2 cup o noodles, 3 nutra grain bars, a strawberry cupcake, a burrito, chips and dip, almost a whole bag of cookies, then for dinner it was 4 tacos. I don't want him to gain too much, and I don't know if there is something wrong that is causing him to be so hungry. I will just monitor him and see how it goes. Other than that news, nothing much new. I am going to an IEP on Tuesday to finalize the decision that Steven will be going to High School next year for 10th grade. I would love for him to stay where he is, but other than my own personal opinions, I believe that he should be where he is age appropriate, I don't ever want him to be different cause of LGS and I don't see a problem with him going to the high school. I just think it's funny...I am not worried too much, I think he will be alright. OK ,well time for me to go get stuff ready for school for him tomorrow, hopefully my next update will be a good one :)

June 17, 2012

Although I have a lot of free time tonight since Steven is sleeping, I am utterly exhausted since school is out and am planning a night of watching tv and crocheting..lol. Just wanted to do a quick update, Steven is doing great on the "O" still, no seizures while he is awake. Sleeping though, he has a couple a night, but some nights none. A couple of weeks ago though, he was clustering so bad that I almost took him to the ER, I called the ped neuro on call at the hospital but never got an answer back, anyways, we just rode it out, the seizures stopped after about an hour and he was fine from then on. Someone mentioned that it was a full moon that night, and it kind of makes me wonder if that doesn't have something to do with it. He hasn't seized like that since, and you better believe that I will be watching on the next full moon to see what happens..lol. Really, though, I am not kidding. Other than that, Steven graduated from middle school last week, he is now officially in High School, almost unbelievable that I have child old enough for high school..lol. I was so proud of him, and even though he really didn't have to make the grades to graduate, it's just the fact that he is still here with me to be ABLE to graduate. So many times I thought I was going to lose him to a seizure, and it's just an amazing feeling to see him walking up and shaking the principals hand and getting his promotion certificate. I still wonder all the what ifs..like, whenever he was a baby, I just KNEW that when he was in high school he would be the quarterback on the football team, and be the most popular guy in school...kind of sad to think about , but I try not to, cause I can't live by the what ifs. In a way I am thankful that he won't be doing the things that I did when I was in high school, or actually a little after high school...lol. I don't have to worry about him driving, or being in the car w/friends...I guess in that way I am considered lucky. Either way, I am so thankful for him, even with his little attitude he has had lately, well, actually a BIG attitude..lol. I am looking forward to next year, and I am praying that the "O" continues to work, it's been over 2 months now. We see the neuro on July 2nd, so maybe she can increase it a little bit at night. OH..and coming up on July 12th..I will be the proud mother of a 15 year old :) Looking forward to many good things to come♥♥

Praying for relief

Aug. 5, 2012

Well, since my last post, we have had some major issues, lots of tears,
frustration and lots and lots of prayers. Steven was put on a new medication called "O", it stopped his seizures, and he is still seizure
free while he is awake. BUT, due to this medicine, he was absolutely
unmanageable. He went into very aggressive rages, tantrums, whatever you want to call it, I just almost couldn't take it anymore. I have a kind of old oak table and chairs, I started with 8 chairs, I am down to 1and another that is barely hanging on, he has thrown them and broke them all. I have holes in my ceiling from the chairs hitting it. My couch that I paid $1800 for, is completely broke on the inside, he
kicked it and ripped the wood out of it. Getting him down on the ground
is almost impossible anymore due to his weight and strength, but of
course me and my dad have to do our best, and we have the bruised to
prove it. My dad has a huge dark purple bruise in the inside of his
upper arm from a twist/pinch from Steven. I was to the point

where I
just cried and really thought about Stevens future. Backing up a little,
after the violence got so out of control I emailed his neurologist andbegged for something to give him, I didn't care what it was, I just couldn't handle it anymore. They prescribed "H", and said it should calm him down, along w/taking him off of "R" and increasing "C". Well, I tried the increases and decreases, but they forgot to call in the "H" over the weekend. That what broke me. I was so looking forward to some relief, and there was nothing. So about a week went by and the neurologist finally got back with me again and said he called it in, but the pharmacy must have lost the RX, so he called it in that day. I also told the neuro that I wanted him OFF of the "O" that was controlling his seizures. I would rather deal with the seizures coming back than the behavior, which was a very hard decision, but I have to do whets best for Steven, Anyways, I decreased the "O" down to 10mg 2x a day, it seemed to help at first, but that was short lived and still no relief. So I started the "H". It has been 4 days now and no relief is in sight. The side effects of this medication are that it could make him even more aggressive if he does not have an actual mental condition, which I think is the direction we are headed and so I decided to stop the "H" starting tonight. I can say that I have had to pay a lot of extra attention to him to get thru this, meaning, more hours in the pool, more coloring time, just more one on one attention...literally until he goes to sleep every night. I am hoping that when he goes back to school in 22 more days, things will change as he won't be stuck with mom 24/7. All I can do is pray and have faith in God that he knows what he is doing and that he will not give more than I can bear. So, I will update again when I can and hopefully it will be a good update, and thanks to those who do read this, it means a lot, and even just for me to be able to write helps so much :)

Praying for a change
Aug. 22, 2012

Well this last week has been awful. I had shared most of this on facebook, but I don't think I fully went into it. Steven has been so mean, so violent it's been almost unbearable. I took him to church 2 weeks ago and when I went into the class to pick him up, I walked into a nightmare. There was a kid who had a Spiderman book, and he let Steven play w/it during church. Well, when the kid left, he took his book and Steven went crazy. I walked in and he was cussing, yelling that he hated church, that everyone was mean to him, he was saying the F word...at church!!!! I calmed him down and went on with my day of fighting w/him. Well a few days ago, we were in the car, my dad was driving. It was after church and he tried to stab my dad with a toy in his neck, so I thought I would crawl into the backseat and calm him down. BIG MISTAKE!! As soon as I got back there, he attacked me, he pulled my hair out in big chunks, I have bald spots on my head, he attacked my legs with his hands, and I have bruised the size of oranges on them. He bit my arm, pinched my arms...it was awful. He kept saying "cry mom, cry" and I wouldn't. I held it in until we got to my grandma's house and burst into tears. He has never attacked me like that before. We have just been trying to keep him busy this week and re direct him when he gets like this. I finally heard back from the neurologist tonight and he is going to take him completely off of the "O"(the med that I was controlling his seizures, but making him crazy) and they are starting a new drug called "P2". I guess this drug is in a new class of drugs and they are very hopeful. I would try anything to make this stop. It's funny cause for so long I was so concerned about just stopping the seizures, but when a medicine causes behavior like I have had to deal with, it has to go, even if it stops the seizures. Hopefully the "P2" will help with both. So with lots of prayers this week, and the med changes, and school finally starting, I am praying for some relief, for me, my dad and for Steven. We will see how it goes, and I will update as soon as I see a change or not.

October 9. 2012

First an update..then some venting..lol!! I took Steven to Los Angeles yesterday to see his neurologist. It was a weird appointment cause there really was no reason for it, weird cause for the first time since we have been going there I really didn't have any issues, which is a good thing!! The neurologist agreed that we can go back up on the "O" just a bit to see how it goes, and we can slowly go off of "C" !!! Then, off of "F" , and then "P"..that's if all goes well. So it was a good visit!! Now to the venting...I posted on facebook tonight about how so many people don't realize how Steven must feel as a disabled child. Many of MY OWN family don't even treat him like a person. I was even told that someone in my family doesn't think that Steven is capable of loving another person. I was literally sick to my stomach to even think that people are so miserable in their own lives that they have to talk bad about Steven. Things get told to others and you know how gossip goes, it gets turned and twisted and by the time it gets back to you it's so much lies it's not even funny. I wanted to scream as I heard what was going around about my son...it just makes me so mad. Yes, I get mad and angry and cry, and yes I put most of my feelings on places like facebook, but that is because most of the people I have on there have a child like Steven and know what I am going thru. When people take what I say out of hand and think I can't handle my son, they are so wrong..I'm sure they have people they talk to, but they don't need the support that a mother w/a special needs child needs. As for the subject of putting Steven in a home, it will NEVER happen. I have heard many people say that I should put him away...how about they send their kids off to a boarding school in some other state...where they don't get to make sure they are cared for, or tuck them into bed every night, or give them a kiss and a hug and tell them how much they love them...they wouldn't do it!! SO why tell me what I should do with my son??? I'm so sick of it....I don't have hate for these people, because I know they are ignorant..but it does get me mad. Oh, I could go on and on and on....but it's not worth it. I'm just glad that they are not in my everyday life and they need to just keep their opinions when it comes to MY son to themselves. I love him, and I will do what God intended for me to do, and that is show Steven love and care for him

November 5. 2012

Well, since my last entry, not much has changed as far as medically with Steven. We decided to decrease the "P" in the afternoon and take him off of "C"...but I have only been able to go as far as half a tab am/pm so far. He is doing pretty good, still having seizures of course, mostly during sleep but that's the ESES of course.. I wish we could stop these. Our goal is to get him off of the "C", then "P", and then "F"..We will have to see how it goes, it's a long road!! Steven is enjoying school, 10th grade, I can't believe it!! There was a time I didn't think he would make it to 10th grade, I am so thankful that he has come so far. He is a smart guy..You wouldn't know it, but I think he has a lot stored in that split brain of his..lol. He amazes me sometimes with the things he says or things he will remember. Anyways, he has adjusted to the change in schools very well, although he does miss his Jr. High teacher (I took him to visit his jr. High on Halloween and he was BEYOND excited to see everyone)..but he LOVES his new teacher and aids. I think he even may have a few friends here!! So I guess no news is good news, for now. His behavior is still something I have to deal with on a daily basis..but, that's just part of LGS and I just have to hang in there. So for now, just a short little update, not much to say...which I guess is a good thing. Thanks to everyone who has been praying for him....and if you get a chance, go back and read my journal..it's amazing to see how far my kiddo has come! :

January 14. 2013

Well, it's been a while, yet again...lol..but I guess that's a good thing, nothing much happening!! Steven continues to have seizures, but nothing new with that!! He is finally off of "C", and we are working on getting "O" back up, but still have to take off some other meds first. I am thinking maybe "P" next?? We see the neuro on Feb 11, so I can't wait to see what her new plan is!! Steven is doing great in school, he loves going and loves his new teacher, and his bus driver!! So for now, just a quick little update...OH..wait, he will be starting hippotherapy, NO..not riding hippos..lol..he will be riding horses for therapy!! I am so excited about this, as his walking is not so good lately. The movement of the horses will help with all of that, so as soon as I get the ok from the place he will start!!! So that's all for now...update you again soon!

Printed in Poland
by Amazon Fulfillment
Poland Sp. z o.o., Wrocław